date night
in a
minivan

date night
in a
minivan

revving up your marriage
after kids arrive

lorilee craker

Revell
Grand Rapids, Michigan

© 2008 by Lorilee Craker

Published by Revell
a division of Baker Publishing Group
P.O. Box 6287, Grand Rapids, MI 49516-6287
www.revellbooks.com

Second printing, March 2008

Printed in the United States of America

Library of Congress Cataloging-in-Publication Data
Craker, Lorilee.
    Date night in a minivan : revving up your marriage after kids arrive
/ Lorilee Craker.
        p.   cm.
    Includes bibliographical references.
    ISBN 978-0-8007-3069-7 (pbk.)
    1. Sex in marriage. 2. Intimacy (Psychology) 3. Parenting. I. Title.
HQ734.C883 2008
306.874—dc22   2007038768

To my parents, Linda and Abe Reimer, for modeling for their children a profound and enduring love, a secure commitment, and the concept that marriage is forever.

A special note to Dad: I miss you, Dad, every day. Thank you for loving Mom so much in your lifetime. I hope you're having the time of your life on the other side. We'll carry the torch until we see you again.

Contents

Acknowledgments

My abiding thanks to the following who assisted in the labor and delivery of this book in some key way:

To the Baker Publishing Group folks, for being such stellar craftsmen and women of words, design, marketing, and editing. Thanks especially to Jennifer Leep, a lovely lady, fine editor, and good pal; Twila Bennett, my fun concert go-to chick; and Dwight Baker, who cares so much about the books he publishes. Baker will always be a family to me.

Thanks to Paula Gibson, Mary Wenger, and Suzie Cross for your hard work on behalf of this book.

To the MOPS folks, especially Beth Lagerborg, Elisa Morgan, and Carol Kuykendall—thank you for your vision for supporting women in a job that can be so isolating and frustrating at times. Being a MOPS member myself, I can appreciate all you do so that your moms are built up and cared for. Mazel tov to you for all of it.

To my beautiful, supportive, ultrasavvy, always-there-for-me Writer's Guild: Ann Byle, Tracy Groot, Shelly

Beach, Julie Johnson, Angela Blyker, Katrina DeMan, Cynthia Beach, and Alison Hodgson. I could babble on for pages about what you have meant to me, individually and collectively, but in short, each one of you is essential. Thank you for building into my life with your graces and your gifts.

To Nancy Rubin, Bonnie Anderson, Becky Wertz-Walker, Lisa Freire, Rachel Arnold, Mary Jo Haab, Sheri Rodriguez, and Emily Grix, for basic, fundamental, girl-friendishness. I am rich because you are my friends!

To Keri Wyatt Kent and Julie Ann Barnhill for knowing exactly what it's like, good and bad, to do this for a living.

And finally, to my family.

To my mom, Linda Reimer, who lost her own soul mate as I was writing this book, thank you for your unselfish love and support.

To my children, Jonah, Ezra, and Phoebe, thanks for sharing your mom with whoever reads this book, and for being the best kids in the whole world!

To Doyle. Thank you for being my companion, my partner, and the love of my life. It hasn't always been easy (has it ever been easy?), but these days it sure does feel good. See you on the dance floor, big guy!

Introduction

My moment of truth was sparked when my husband dropped the baby. To his credit, she kind of lurched out of his arms, headfirst onto the hardwood floor. It wasn't so much that he dropped the poor child on her head, but rather my reaction: it wasn't pretty. My maternal mother bear thing reared its grizzly head. That, coupled with an almighty knee-jerk reaction, resulted in the following heated, high-decibel exchange taking place above the fray of a squalling infant:

"What is wrong with you? How could you do that?" (Moi.)

"C'mon—she, like, pitched forward and I couldn't catch her. She's fine!" (Him.)

"You always let her fall!" (Gulp. Me again.)

"I do not always let her fall. You've let her fall too!" (Him, getting mad.)

"Not like you! You overestimate her ability to sit still!" (Yikes. That would be me, out of control and grasping at straws.)

Of course, we were comforting our sniffling little one as we battled over who had the most accurate appraisal of our eight-month-old's large motor skills. It was ludicrous, and about five minutes later I felt like the diva of all buffoons. But the incident did crystallize a thought: *me and my man just haven't been getting along like we were before we added our darling third child to the Craker Clan.*

At the base of my freak-out was the lurking little thought that Doyle—though a great hands-on dad by any standard—wasn't quite to be trusted to take care of the baby, not 100 percent trusted, anyway. After all, he wouldn't be giving her a mother's care, my care, now would he? And therein lay the rub. I was ashamed to admit it, even to myself. Me, who always talked big about equality and coparenting, blah, blah, blah—I was guilty of "maternal gatekeeping," not letting Dad fully engage in the nitty-gritty of nurturing duties.

That was just one issue that had cropped up since Baby 3. There was also an exacerbated case of the ol' Time-Off Tug-o-War too. With new and intense demands on our time, both of us were pulling on our ends of the rope for a pocket of freedom. Don't get me wrong: we were gaga over our baby girl, and pretty crazy about her big brothers too, but with her arrival came new challenges to our relationship.

I read once that with each child added to a family, there's that much more stress between the parents, and that much more distance to cross to being close again. I believe it. What's stressful about raising those darling little cherubs we love and adore? Well, for starters, how about the never-ending labor it takes just to keep an active, just-walking turbo tot unscathed and germ free? Often at the end of a day filled with basic child preservation, like most moms I need a break in the worst way. Unfortunately, on such days my husband will end up having an equally harried day at work, and he needs a break too. Harassed, strung out, and stick-a-fork-in-me-I'm-done *done*, we are not our best selves when we greet each other at 5:30 p.m. On such a crazy day we can be worn out, unhinged, and just trying to keep all the most important balls in the air, at least until bedtime. Yet the kids still need to be fed, bathed, and generally nurtured, so guess where our marriage relationship ranks on the totem pole of life? Low, people, low.

We need to figure out ways to rise above the mayhem that comes with family life and still care for each other, and cultivate stronger ties to get us through the crazy times.

Don't even get me started about romance! Though our baby is adopted—i.e., no physical recovery—we still are surprisingly tired, irritated, and disconnected, not exactly the poster couple for parenthood and passion that we had hoped to become in the wake of my book *We Should Do This More Often*.

Clearly, Mom (me) and Dad (Doyle) need to get it goin' on again, but do other couples with little ones face the same sticky wickets? I talked to my girlfriends, MOPS

(Mothers of Preschoolers) pals, and other mommy amigos, and picked their brains about the whole topic of how preschoolers can be hazardous to their parents' love lives. Everyone chimed in, kvetching about the difficulty of maintaining warm friendship with one's man—never mind anything hotter—when raising a pile of youngsters in the way they should go. Several hot-topic buttons were pushed, and the themes began to gel. It became clear I needed to write my next book on keeping the marriage fires stoked while parenting preschoolers. Crammed with stories, humor, and road-tested tips from my pals and me, not to mention studded with research and interviews, I hope it will help to rev up my own and other moms' marriages.

As parents, we can and often do spend eighteen years trying to find each other again, which is a shame. True companionship shouldn't be rocket science, even when the house is filled with tiny interlopers who want you to cater to their every whim. This is your handbook, and mine, for reclaiming friendship, teamwork, and yes folks, vava voom. There must be vava voom!

Is it possible to get along famously with the father of your children, even when those same tots present no end of challenges to your relationship?

Can Ma and Pa work out their parenting differences and bargain for the time off, together and alone, that they so desperately need?

Can hurdling these kiddie-related obstacles actually bond a woman and her husband in a way they've never even dreamed of?

What do you think?

Yes!

Mom and Dad can get it goin' on again. You and your main man can rev up your marriage, along with that beautiful minivan, and recapture some of that pre-kid dating buzz. Put your key in the ignition, my friend, and together we'll figure out how.

1

Mom's the Bad Guy and Dad's the Softie, or Vice Versa

Getting a handle on your different discipline styles

Clashes over discipline are a surefire way to get your relationship caught in a buzz saw. When Mom and Dad aren't on the same page in terms of how to rein in those bedeviling little angels—and often they're not—everyone can get caught in the fray, even the dog (more about that later).

Doyle and I actually don't butt heads over this one too much, although it certainly crops up from time to time. We tend to go loco over different kiddie infractions, though, which can cause just a wee bit of stress and discord. Just a wee bit.

Say the boys have been shedding clothes, socks, costumes, toys, markers, and other detritus all day long.

The carpet is no longer visible to the naked eye by the time they are done for the day. The baby, of course, doesn't have any obligation to pick up her stuff, which means usually I do it, if anyone. She only weighs eighteen pounds, but she is a world-class, gold-standard mess maker, as all toddler newbies are. So the house is trashed, and I'm steamed.

Why? If I were the one running herd that day, I may have, at various junctures, instructed the demolition derby of two that socks do not belong in the magazine rack, or hockey equipment anywhere but the equipment bag. That if a worn-once rugby shirt ends up on the love seat, the dog, who coolly disregards the do-not-sit-on-the-love-seat-or-die rule, will dispense dozens of white hairs all over the shirt, rendering it into laundry. But if I'm not there, or working in the basement, these things can and do happen.

"Umm, could you tell them to pick up their stuff once in awhile?" I will say pleasantly, trying not to sound like a big nag.

"Oh, uh, yeah, I just figured they could do it at bedtime," D says, not missing a beat from his remote patrol.

"It actually is bedtime, and they are already on another floor of the house," I say, a little less pleasantly, because, like many, many childrearing conflicts, we've had it a billion times. I want to mention that, had he seen fit to throw out a "Hey guys, could you throw your dirty clothes in the basement?" or maybe a little "Let's clear a path for travelers en route to the kitchen so as to avoid grave bodily injury," it would have possibly reduced the stupefying amount of laundry to be done. I want to, but

I don't. I want to roll my eyes and sigh, but that would just be plain naughty.

I have relatively low standards, folks, so when the clutter gets to me, you know it ain't pretty. But that's a stickler where I'm the uptight one. I'm sure you've been in my shoes a thousand times, with you and your co-parent man not being on the same page when it comes to any number of childrearing issues, big and small. And you also know that there are equally as many instances where you are the mellower party and your husband wants more of a goose-stepping response to his notion of obedience. For example, bedtime hassles bug the living daylights out of Doyle while I have the attitude of "Hey, it's a classic struggle and we're making some progress. Let's call it good for now and keep trying."

Why is it so hard to see eye to eye sometimes on how to deal with the munchkins when they've gone astray in some way? For one thing, often Mom or Dad doesn't even view a given behavior as *being* particularly astray, while their mate looks at it as completely off-target.

So often parenting styles can clash more than they mesh, causing all kinds of friction. Why are we so different when it comes to how we discipline our kids? First, we are totally different people, poles apart, so dissimilar that even the tiniest baby picks up on the singular approach of each of his parents. "For a baby, mothers and fathers are different from the beginning," wrote the late Fred Rogers. "They look different, sound different, smell different, feel different, hold their babies differently and react differently to their babies' cues and signals. Doesn't it seem natural that they should, as time goes by, have differences in the ways they raise their children?"[1]

Amen, Mr. Rogers, you wise, dear man. That's the first step in untangling ourselves and our relationships from the snare of polarizing battles, to get it through our thick skulls that Mom and Dad are going to be unlike each other when it comes to discipline. "No husband and wife were ever raised in exactly the same ways by their parents, and all of us bring echoes from our own childhoods to the task of raising our children when it's our turn."[2] Sometimes those discipline philosophies, etched by our backgrounds, are hidden until the moment of truth arrives and Baby makes three. Then Mom is appalled when Dad regards Junior, who is pinching his baby sister or loudly chucking toys against the wall, as "just being a boy." And Dad is dazed when his bride, who he thought was such an easygoing person, turns into the Sugar Nazi and won't let their toddler have one piece of birthday cake at her cousin's birthday. One piece! He can hardly believe it.

It's like Mom and Dad have to get to know each other all over again when they have kids, isn't it? That's what the parents we'll hear from below faced as their latent discipline styles came to the forefront: *Who is this person I am married to? Because I never knew he/she would act this way when it came to training and raising our kids!*

Let's listen to some moms and dads air their differences and then we'll have a little coffee klatch, you and me, and figure out some functional, real-world ways for moms and dads with different parenting styles to form a united front.

Dish Panel

Her Mode: sweet talk; His Mode: crack down

Trina: Frankly, I can't believe that Neil and I, who used to agree on just about everything, could be so far apart on this of all things.

I guess I do want to be the softie. But he can be so hard on the boys. I don't see why he needs to point it out when the boys do something as harmless as holding their forks wrong. A lot of times I feel they are just kids being kids. If they fight when they are in the car, I'll kind of sweet-talk them to stop before cracking down. Neil would just say, "No more arguing. You're going to bed as soon as we get home."

I like to talk through problems, which Neil loathes. He issues commands and then expects everyone to fall in step. I'm frustrated and tired of making comments or giving Neil a dirty look when I think he's being too tough.

That's the worst, isn't it? When one person is black and white about things, and the other one sees only gray? Hmmm . . . wonder where I've seen that scenario play out before? Oh yes. Just about every day!

Neil: I'm always the designated bad guy.

A parent has to make decisions even though they are unpleasant, even though the kid cries. Trina gives in because she doesn't want the children to be mad at her. Wyatt (4) has her wrapped around his finger. If I punish him for talking back, he runs to Mommy and she leaps to his defense, telling me to stop being mean to him. What kind of message does this send? Trina's idea of discipline is to try reasoning with the boys ten times, then she loses it. The next thing you know, she and I are mad at each other.

Her Mode: "She's just a baby"; His Mode: "She's got to learn right from wrong"

Sarah: My husband Rob and I are first-time parents of a fourteen-month-old girl, Reece. We have pretty different parenting styles, particularly when the baby is doing something she shouldn't be.

For example, when Reece hits me in the face, I'll tell her in a normal voice that she shouldn't do that or that we don't hit in our house, catch her hands to prevent her doing it again, and try to distract her and move on to something else. My husband is more likely to get angry and use an angry tone of voice, and/or put Reece (crying) in her crib for a time-out. This is absolutely ridiculous to me! She's a baby, for Pete's sake, and I think he is making things much worse. This is very upsetting to me, as I hate hearing her scream. I feel kind of resentful of Rob, and

I wonder how I ended up with someone so strict to my baby. When I confront him, he gets really upset and says I don't respect him. Well, sometimes I don't. And that scares me a little.

Ugh! This is so common, to have one parent, often but not always the dad, take a hard line on an issue that his partner thinks requires a softer approach. Poor Sarah. (And poor Rob too.)

Her Mode: respond; His Mode: react

Deanna: I think Aaron and I have finally come to a middle ground on our disciplining styles, and what a relief that is, I can't even tell you.

Aaron is more of a "my way or the highway" guy and reacts within seconds of our daughter doing something wrong by yelling and freaking out. I am more laid back, with a philosophy of "three strikes and you're outta there," a firm "no!" with an explanation, and a time-out in the naughty chair (thanks, Super Nanny) if those things don't work with Bettina, our three-year-old.

I found it so infuriating that he was always yelling at Betts, though I must say he has never spanked her in anger. I am always the calmer party, and I usually ignore a tantrum—I read somewhere that you should do that—or distract Bettina with another activity.

Our relationship was affected by his outbursts because I felt kind of let down and sad that he wasn't as laid back as he used to be before we had kids.

We had a very rude awakening when Bettina had a tantrum one morning and Aaron, not a morning person, couldn't handle it and both of them were yelling at each other. I myself was very tempted to jump in and start yelling—at Aaron, for being such a jerk and not having the parenting skills to handle our daughter's childish tantrums like a grown-up. I just left the room and prayed for calm and peace at my house. I can't stand yelling, and I just don't think it makes Bettina respect us at all, which is what I want for her. And I want her to grow up and know the consequences of her actions.

Finally, when things settled, we talked about the double tantrum and how upset it had left us all. Even our dog Caboodle was upset by it!

We decided we had to find a compromise, because he felt I was too lax and I felt he was way too freaked out about everything.

What's great here is that Aaron and Deanna actually sorted through their feelings a bit and talked about their different parenting styles. That's the first step to making positive changes!

Her Mode: bad cop; His Mode: "Can't we all just get along?"

Erin: I am the bad cop and Frankie isn't even the good cop; he doesn't do any policing at all.

If Gabe is acting up, Frankie says "No, Gabe" or "Stop that, Gabe" but never follows through. Gabe (3) now pays little or no attention to his dad, and just turns away and says, 'Whatever.' Frankie really has to step up to the plate and learn how to actually be a parent in times like that. It frustrates me so much and makes me lose respect for Frank."

Nora: Somebody around here has got to take the job and be a parent.

I've told Louis many, many times that he has to be consistent and he has to follow through! If he's not going to do either, then he needs to not say anything at all. Our Meredith has had him wrapped around her finger for years, and she's only four. Sad thing, he doesn't even see it, even though I've pointed it out to him many times. Guys are just clueless sometimes."

His Mode: "Give peace a chance"; Her Mode: "Peace doesn't accomplish my discipline goals"

Oren: Pam says "peaceful" can be mistaken for "passive" but I disagree. It's still better than all that yelling.

Our kids are now five and three, and my wife and I have been wrestling with these issues for about five years, give or take. Her fuse is much shorter overall, though she was much less inclined to let the kids "cry it out" when they were babies. Pam grew up in a home that was characterized by lots of fighting and drama, and my upbringing was so much more peaceful. We have very different ideas about discipline that are most obvious when the kids need us most.

Family stuff is huuuuuge when it comes to how we parent our own kids. In chapter 5 we'll delve deeper into how to "retouch" those old family portraits so both Mom and Dad understand each other better.

Get It Goin' On (Otherwise Known as GIGO)

A note about "Get It Goin' On," henceforth to be called "GIGO." This section of the book will occur last in every chapter, usually after my "Dish Panel" of friends, readers, and passersby chime in with their own joys and concerns about a particular topic. After the problem is outlined and real moms (and the occasional dad) have their say, it's time to present solutions, answers, ideas—basically, keys to unlocking those stuck minivan doors in our journeys with our husbands. Hopefully, GIGO will give you take-it-to-the-bank-and-cash-it tips for revving up the engines of your stalled love life.

Whew! The moms and dads who aired their different parenting styles in our Dish Panel—and revealed how those differences make them cranky—were so honest it was a little scary. I don't know about you but I feel a bit singed, like I've gotten too close to a pan of something that's burning. (I burn a lot of food so I know what I'm talking about here!)

There's that acrid smell in the air; you know, "acrid" is from the same root word as "acrimonious." Not a happy word, ladies. In fact, the antonym is "harmonious." But as we've heard from our fellow moms, and as we ourselves know, clashing discipline styles is one scorching, hot-button issue.

How do we get from too hot to handle to a place of more calm, more agreement, and more sweetness altogether? It won't be easy, but let's try throwing some cool water on the fire first. When the smoke clears, we can see eye to eye and start from there. How do we douse the fractiousness this issue sparks? Baby steps, as always, but before anything is resolved we have no choice but to lower those torches—and defenses.

Let Down Your Defenses by Understanding Each Other

Let's talk about that Sugar Nazi mom again. If her husband got the inside scoop on this seemingly overboard response, he'd understand that his bride has a reason for being so hostile toward the sweet stuff. As a child, Miss Anti-Sugar was given gallons of pop to drink, and almost unlimited access to candy and sweet treats by her busy, distracted mother, who had eight kids to worry about. The result is that she has endured nightmarish visits to the dentist over the years, plus has uncomfortable childhood memories of feeling half-sick sometimes from eating too much junk food. She's a first-time mom, which means Susie Sans Sugar desperately wants to be the best mom she can be, cracking the whip on any granule of sweetener she comes across. And yeah, she's over the top, but her husband doesn't help matters by making jabs at her stance.

Sometimes getting at the root of those hard-liner issues, connecting the dots with each other, can be the first step in letting go of those prickly defensive attitudes.

Take Neil and Trina. Both suspect that each simply wants the other to give in to his or her approach—which makes both of them throw up walls. When she tells Neil to be more nurturing, he says, "You just want me to be like you."

Because this couple—once so gaga over each other they made everyone around them go into sugar shock (speaking of sugar)—won't even peek at each other's point of view, their relationship is starting to warp. Both Neil and Trina have dug in their heels and want to be right, darn it! We've all been there a time or two—*today.* We all want to be right, and for some of us it's more important to be right than to have a caring, respectful relationship.

But the defenses have to come down, or all is lost. I'm not being a drama queen here: all is lost when we refuse to meet each other halfway. But how, oh how, is that possible? Check out these next few ideas and see if one or two don't neutralize some of your heated discipline battles.

Find the "Tugs"

Since the way we parent is directly linked to the kind of parenting we received, recognizing this is key to understanding each other on a whole new level. Sugar Mama, obviously, is hugely affected by her own mom's lackadaisical nutrition policies, and vows to be "better."

With me and Doyle, I now know (took me only eight years) his instant snit over bedtime battles is rooted in his childhood bedtimes, which were smooth, orderly affairs. "I would never have come downstairs twice after being put in bed," he has said. "I doubt very much I would have even dared come out of my bedroom once after being told to stay there."

When our lads (especially the five-year-old, a mulish child if there ever was one) come downstairs for "one kiss" or "one drink," it has the immediate effect of making Doyle feel ineffective and impotent as a dad. I get that. Finally I do, after feeling a little irked a thousand times because he wasn't more blasé about an extra hug and a kiss and the occasional glass of milk. Those childhood roots have a way of wrapping around us, and when something feels wrong—in Doyle's case, when his boys weren't as compliant as he was expected to be—we feel a big tug.

I feel no tug on this issue, although of course I am frustrated that things don't go more smoothly some nights. But when I finally got Doyle's tug, I could see why he was bent out of shape about it (i.e., "tugged").

How do we figure out those tugs before they yank the rug out from under us? One idea is to draw a genogram, or a psychological family tree that describes family members across several generations, outlining the strengths and weaknesses of each person. If you think your man will balk at any hint of psychobabble (mine would), just call it something else:

"I read somewhere that we can really understand each other better by talking about our parents and how they treated us." And maybe . . .

"I want us to get along better and get each other more in terms of how we discipline Mason. I really think this might help."

Even a casual conversation about the stuff our parents did well and what they messed up on could be like gold as far as grasping each other's discipline approaches.

Recognizing why we act a certain way, of course, is not the same as actually changing the way we act (if it needs to be changed). But still, a little bit of empathy goes a long way toward bringing down the heat and tension over discipline.

Sometimes we don't even know what causes a knee-jerk reaction. But it helps to put it on the table anyway. It takes big guts to say:

"I am not sure exactly why, but I have a hard time having Normie be mad at me, so I guess I do let things slide a bit too much with him sometimes."

Or . . .

"I wish I could change, but sometimes I just yell first and ask questions later."

Vulnerability can be the conduit of grace. If we let our guard down and own up to some of our failings, we give an inch. And then what often happens is our beloved gives an inch too. And inch by inch we tunnel our way back to each other as lovers and romantic partners, not just parents pitted against each other in a never-ending skirmish over bedtimes and tantrums and sugar.

Disarm Him, but Don't Throw a Grenade at the Guy

Deanna found a way to get her point across in a way that disarmed Aaron instead of making him madder. "I showed Aaron an article about how tantrums are normal at Bettina's age, and how her emotions were just too big for her to handle. He read also that yelling at a tantrum is like pouring fuel on the fire. Somehow reading it in a magazine went down much better than me telling him I had read it there! I also made sure I wasn't like, 'I am right and this proves it.' I tried to take the approach that we were both in this together—which we are—and we both need all the help we can get."

Remember, Dads Are from Mars, and Moms Are from Venus (or Pluto, or Someplace Other Than Mars)

Like Mr. Rogers said, each parent is going to come at discipline from another place altogether. For instance, moms, especially if they are around the house a lot more, often know what works, and they intend to follow it. And we feel more responsible and usually more worried about how other people—relatives, friends, preschool teachers—view our offspring's behavior. Dads, conversely, are like Teflon when it comes to the comments and scrutiny of other people. They just don't care as much when little Sasha is showing her Sunday school class her big girl panties, or Pedro is picking his nose at the preschool Christmas program.

The upshot? It's always good to think about how we are different as men and women, and how those innate distinctions infiltrate our parenting journey from the beginning. With a little more understanding, a bit more neutral negotiating, and some give and take, we can disarm, defuse, and actually move closer to being on the same team.

Talk More, Using Your Big Girl Words

Deb dislikes the way Mike is always telling her to lighten up. Who wouldn't? When you tell someone to lighten up, you may as well go on and delineate all the ways they are repressed, uptight, shrewish, and generally a big fat stick in the mud. Telling the love of your life, then, to lighten up is bad form and leads to more friction, conflict, and that funny burning smell.

Also no-no's:

"Do you have to be such a jerk about it?"

"Way to handle that, Einstein."

"If you did it my way, everything would be much better around here."

"Grow up!"

Yeah, you get my point. But in the heat of a tiff, it's so easy to blow a gasket when what's really needed is a cooler head and a better choice of words. A clear communiqué is important when any problem crops up in marriage, especially when it comes to parenting. Usually women don't tell our guys what we need from them. We just stew about it, snap at them sarcastically, or maybe even turn into blithering banshees.

Take our pal Trina. She has to tell Neil, "This is what I need from you," and then explain why she needs it in black and white, no fuzziness. "I need to sit down and figure out how we can find some middle ground in our discipline styles," she says. "There's got to be a way to compromise here." She admits she's still in get-mad-first-and-ask-questions-later mode.

Here's a news flash that won't surprise you: most guys are genuinely unaware of why some point of parenting is so incredibly important to their wives. If you point out, for example, that you don't want Otis eating a Snickers bar at four o'clock because then he won't eat dinner, your husband may think again before handing over the candy just so he can have some peace and watch ESPN. Then again, you may be able to work out a little deal. Instead of a candy bar, would one tube of yogurt be the end of the world? No? Well, work it out then instead of having a cow next time Otis isn't hungry because Daddy gave him a snack!

Also, instead of immediately going for the little jab or the big slam, we have to learn to ask for help, as in, "I'm really struggling with how to . . .

> set limits at bedtime . . .
>
> keep the house tidier . . .
>
> balance your harder/softer approach with my softer/harder style."

By asking for the man's input, you actually draw him into the process. You essentially make room for him in the coach's corner, so to speak. Criticizing him only pulls the two of you farther apart.

Sarah uses a brilliant idea to talk things through and build teamwork. She sits down with her husband every so often and the twosome actually write down the top three things that make them most unglued when it comes to their four-year-old son's behavior. Her list?

Fighting him over what to wear that day

Mealtime battles ("I get panicked when he won't eat. It drives me nuts," she said.)

Whining

Bryan's list is completely different:

Talking back

Wanting to leave the table two minutes after they start eating

Unbuckling his car seat

"We've had some real 'aha' moments during these meetings," she said. "He never really knew that me and Braden struggled so much in the morning over clothes, or that sometimes it put me in a bad mood for the rest of the day."

They brainstorm about the consequences for each infraction and come up with compromises both can live with. Because they now know what rankles their partner, they can watch for it and have each other's back when Braden acts up. "We actually have a plan of sorts, which is way better than just being in reaction mode all the time and getting testy with each other."

Talking through things more can make your discipline issues become a puzzle to solve together, as a team. Go team!

You May Be More Alike Than You Think, So Keep Talking

Instead of blowing your differences out of proportion, try, try, and then try some more to focus on what you do have in common. Think the list is too short to mention? This little exercise may surprise you, like it did with Deanna and Aaron. "We both believe in time-outs and in Bettina following the rules of the house. Plus we both can't stand it when she doesn't pick up her toys or when she is unkind to anyone."

That's a start. From your short list you can also chat about parenting ideals you do share.

You want kids who follow their dreams.

And obey the law. (That's kind of bare minimum, but you can see where I'm going.)

Your heart's desire is for your child to grow up and work hard and take responsibility for her actions.

You would both be tickled pink if little Howie found a profession he was passionate about and surrounded himself with great friends who treated him well.

The longer you daydream about your mutual parenting philosophies, the more you may think, *Hey, we're at least in the same chapter, if not on the same page.* Thus fortified by the knowledge that your big-picture values and goals are actually similar, you'll feel much perkier about solving those pesky little differences.

Aaron and Deanna were able to loosen up the gridlock in their parenting, finally realizing that neither of their styles was all right or all wrong. "We have slowly learned to give and take more with each other," Deanna says. "We now handle Bettina's tantrums differently, with us not just ignoring her, but not giving in to her demands either. For other issues, like when Bettina would grab a toy from her baby brother or something, we decided to give her one chance only and then give her a time-out—one time-out, mind you, not three!—if she still misbehaved. Aaron still has to work on his temper, and I have to stiffen my spine and lay down the law with Betts, but at least now that we are starting to be on the same page, things are happier and healthier at our house."

Warm Is Good

Sometimes blending different childrearing ideas can make both Mom and Dad feel like they've been pureed themselves, speaking of blending. And as much as we want to be right—and that desire never goes away completely—we have to remember we are crushing the one we love. Remember? The same guy who made you weak in the knees when his hand brushed yours, once upon a time? He's the same guy with whom you're in a logjam, deadlocked about how to discipline those kids you both adore.

So take a cue from Aaron and Deanna, who have gotten it through their admittedly thick skulls that they have to start working together on this little project involving the shaping and molding of their precious offspring.

Drop your guard, even a little, and see if he doesn't drop his too. Talk about what bugs you instead of freaking out about the same deal time after time. And keep in mind you are probably closer to being on the same page than you ever imagined.

2

The Time-Off Tug-o-War

Who's cutting the breaks
around here anyway?

Here's some full disclosure, ladies, because you girls are my peeps and I need to be honest with you: the matter of time off and who gets it and when is the stickiest wicket in my own marriage by a country mile. And speaking of country miles, Doyle is a boy from the boondocks who becomes like the proverbial caged animal when he doesn't get regular escapes from our city home to the wide-open spaces he loves. He doesn't consider hunting and fishing his hobbies, but rather elemental activities that feed the very core of his being. In other words, if he doesn't get time off to hunt and fish, he's not a happy guy.

This burning desire to be at one with nature, freezing his tokhes off in the wee hours of the morning on some tree stand in some clump of forest somewhere, wasn't really a problem before we had kids. Well, I still thought it was kind of a lame way to spend time, even back then.

Let me back up a little. If you know me at all from my books or articles, you know that I'm not exactly the rural type. Although I did grow up visiting and loving my grandparents' wheat farm in southern Manitoba. And once in awhile I enjoy sitting for a spell on my mother-in-law's glider rocker, listening to the birds and watching the horses in the pasture. I don't mind a little nature. But in moderation, mind you.

My dad was a city guy, an urban bookseller who appreciated the creature comforts civilization had to offer, such as warmth and dryness. Our home was in the city, and his bookstore was downtown. So when I flitzed into Doyle's family, a city girl to the core, I was in for some surprises when it came to how Craker menfolk liked to spend their free time. Why would any sane person, I thought, get up before the blessed birds to sit for endless hours in the rain and snow, with no company save the squirrels, hoping a four-legged furry something would amble on by?

Fishing isn't that bad, except for the worms. (Remind me to tell you about the time I went trout fishing in a river with Doyle, wearing waders and the whole nine yards, and a night-crawler fell down my top. Yeah, I went a bit catatonic, and after the worm was retrieved, slightly bananas.) But hunting is something I have never really understood.

Therein lies the rub, which has rubbed our relationship raw at times over the past fourteen and a half years. Doyle has an almost primal urge to spend hours and hours of our family's time doing something I don't really comprehend, and sometimes I resent having to make sacrifices on my end so he can go out and do it.

With each subsequent child, the "pie" of family time, time together, and time for individual pursuits was sliced even thinner. Yes, I did come to realize over the years that Doyle truly, foundationally needed enough time to get out in the woods and do his thing. But after a week of caring for the kids during the day and working most evenings on my writing, I sorely need some downtime as well. At the very least I need him around to share, as Alanna mentions below, the emotional and disciplinary load of parenting.

Doyle and I are not alone in this struggle. Plenty of you go head-to-head almost daily over who is more entitled to the little free time you manage to whittle out of your busy schedules.

Let's talk about that pie thing again. The more kids you have, the less time you have for yourself to play. And you know what they say about all work and no play. It's crucial to chisel out pockets of time for one's own recreation and rejuvenation.

Experts say that having time alone—away from each other and without the demands or responsibility of child-care—is actually a vital way to nourish a marriage. We usually don't recognize that taking time alone has anything to do with how strong our marriage is, but truly it has everything to do with it. What's obvious is that both Mom and Dad need to step away from the family fray on a regular basis. "I am a full-time stay-at-home mom of Holden (two and a half years old) and my husband works eight to five Monday through Friday," says Maggie. "I am still working toward balance for both of us to have time off. I tend to feel entitled to a break after a full day yet also realize my husband needs breaks too."

Who's getting the breaks becomes the big question.

Who's getting the breaks becomes the big question, and sometimes that's hard to tell. The lines are blurry on this issue, as in the case of so many vital matters. Listen to Jamie break down her and her husband's "time cards" and their struggle to figure out who's punching in when—and why:

If we are talking general, hang-out-with-your-friends kind of "time off," then my husband gets more than I do. I am part of a MOPS group, and two days a month I spend a few hours scrapbooking/stamping or playing Bunco with "my girls." My DH (dear husband) is a football coach, and has been on a "coaches retreat" every summer—which is at least four days off with a tiny bit of business. He also spends many weekends at ball games (sometimes we get to "tag along" but not often).

We have talked about it and argued about it, and I have just accepted that I cannot change it. I think he "gets" more time because somehow that is the nature of his job, and it is important that, in the case of the coaches retreat, the coaches are comfortable and "bonded" with one another because of the intensity of their jobs. I did tell him, though, that it would never be "fair" (don't you hate that word?) until they started offering a coaches' wives retreat, with just four days of late night giggling, spa treatments, and getting to know one another. After all, we have to "work" just as hard as they do—and perhaps we even sacrifice a little more.

Jamie's wishing out loud for a coaches' wives retreat is so true to real life. But she's right; don't get hung up on what's fair or you are in trouble. I have started down this road before, thinking thoughts such as, *Why does Doyle get to take off for five hours each Saturday to hunt, when I wouldn't dream of suggesting I go scrapbooking, shopping, or out with my pals for that amount of time every week?*

That's a bad road, girls. It only leads to resentment and arguing, certainly nothing productive. And it really torpedoes the whole "keep no record of wrongs" idea, found all over the Bible but specifically in 1 Corinthians 13. The truth remains that so often, there is a decidedly lopsided element to that time-off pie, and Dad almost always gets the bigger piece.

But why? Certainly one aspect at work here is mother's guilt. Why on earth would we ever want to leave our precious children, or even need a break? "Sometimes, honestly, I simply fall into the trap that he is the provider and I am the nurturer and he needs a getaway more than I do," says Jamie. "I even feel a little guilty for wanting to be away from my family. But I believe there needs to be more of a balance."

Balance—now that's a much more beautiful word than "fair." After all, we all know life is not fair, but we can work toward more balance and equilibrium. Did you know that the antonym for equilibrium is "unsteadiness"? "Unsteady" just about describes me when I am craving a respite from my responsibilities as a mom, when it seems as if everyone and the dog wants a piece of me and I have no pieces left to give. "Wobbly" is another way to put it, and some days "loony" fits too.

Our guys feel the same way when they don't get that downtime. Later, in GIGO, we'll hammer out some functional strategies for finding this elusive balance. But first, let's listen to the dish ladies blab all about the Time-Off Tug-o-War in their own homes.

Dish Panel

Betsy: Yes, I would like more time off, but don't get it because I feel guilty about as much time off as I do have. What's misleading is that I feel like I am always on duty more because I am the stay-at-home mom.

I probably end up getting more time off, because I schedule things ahead of time. He tends to get a few minutes here and there, though, because it's easier for him to walk out of the house and into the barn. I don't have that luxury.

Lisa: I feel a bit guilty by daring to imagine myself fleeing the comfort of my home and leaving the safety and well-being of my children to their father.

My husband Dan definitely gets more time off— primarily by taking golf trips with his group of friends I fondly refer to as "the girls." One of the reasons he does take time off is that he *plans* to; I don't.

It's not that I don't think I deserve a little time away, but I truly have the life I have always wanted:

being a stay-at-home mom who is active in her children's school and at our church. So, that being said, I feel a bit guilty by daring to imagine myself fleeing the comfort of my home and leaving the safety and well-being of my children to their father.

See the next chapter on maternal gatekeeping!

Shannon: When our daughter was an infant, I didn't have realistic expectations of what motherhood would entail. . . . But the loss of freedom, the burden of twenty-four-hour responsibility, and the sleep deprivation made me extremely envious of my husband.

The other part is *expectations*. This was key for me. Instead of seeing the blessing of being a twenty-four-hour mom to my child, I saw all that I'd lost by giving up my career and freedom. For us, this was made even worse by a recent move to a new area (i.e., no friends, no church support) and being in a lower income where we shared one car (i.e., when hubby's at work, I'm stuck at home). If we had sat down before Naomi was born or shortly thereafter and discussed these feelings and expectations, I would've enjoyed her first six months much more, not to mention having been a better wife.

Alanna: Time off?!

We both work all the time, just at different locations—me at home, he at the credit union. But when he gets a day or week off, it is a little like time off for me in that I feel like I'm not carrying so much of the daily emotional and discipline loads at home.

But do we (moms) ever have time off? Even if I go out for a few hours, day or evening, I still make sure that there's something for everyone to eat. I need to communicate who had how long a nap, therefore they should go to bed at _:_ _ p.m. I make sure that all details have been communicated and call out a few last-minute instructions. It's rare that I can just leave the house for more than an hour and not feel responsible. I'm not complaining—it's just how it is.

We have time off when we go on dates with each other, when he goes out with the boys, or I go out with the girls. Rick goes out with the guys on average once every two months and I have a girls' night out approximately once every three or four months. I don't go out as often because I might get my outing during the day—coffee/playdates with friends. Sometimes time just slips away from me before I realize that I need an evening out.

Erin: In our case, keeping accounts would be absolutely disastrous.

We're both self-employed, and we're both working our tails off and trying to be good parents too. Neither of us fears that the other will go overboard with demands to get away (because so far, neither of us has been guilty of that). So we take opportunities as they come and as they make sense. Sometimes he gets more time off and sometimes I do, and in the end it all works out.

Laura: I am very blessed to have a husband who acknowledges my need to get out of the house and away from the three kids periodically.

I scrapbook at least once a month for about six hours with a group of friends from church. My husband is a pastor, and his schedule is a bit more flexible than most dads. He would love to play more golf, etc. but spends most of his downtime with us. We have found that we truly have more fun and relax more when we have the opportunity to discover new adventures together. Sometimes this comes in going shopping for plants, looking around a local greenhouse that grows orchids, sightseeing in our town, or adventuring to a new location for just a few hours or a few days.

Sometimes we each feel like we need a bigger break. I do occasionally get jealous when he gets to go to a conference by himself or a retreat just for pastors, and I get left at home for three days alone with our children. Once I am done with nursing our ten-month-old, I will be able to run off more easily for weekend retreats, etc.

Julie: I feel a little like I have to prove my value now that I'm not bringing home any green stuff.

I definitely feel as though my husband gets more time off. I worked for the first two years of my oldest son's life. I made so many statements that began "If I can quit teaching when our second is born . . ." You name it, he was gonna get it—home-cooked meals every night (no more Hamburger Helper–type cheating), organized/clean home, help with his own construction business, more time and attention paid to him, sell all of the girlie toys from my childhood on eBay (we had two very masculine boys and those Strawberry Shortcakes were never going to see the light of day). In essence, I was soooooo desperate to quit work that I convinced him I would be superwoman if I could quit. So now I am in the midst of my first year as a "super hero." I think if I would ask for more help he would do it, but I'm going to let the hoopla of quitting die down a bit first. Don't get me wrong—I am thrilled to be home with my little guys, but I feel a little like I have to prove my value now that I'm not bringing home any green stuff.

As you just read, lots of moms struggle with the Time-Off Tug-o-War. It has so many components, but a big one is that we moms don't know how to walk away from hearth and home without feeling guilty or responsible. And we often view our husband's time off with jealousy, even though there's probably a good way to hammer out a plan for both parties to get away here and there. Next check out some ideas that will hopefully help you figure out how to do just that.

GIGO

Remember, His "Day Job" Ain't Playtime

"Sometimes it's hard to not consider some of my husband's time spent working on the job as time off," says

Betsy. Ann concurs: "It's hard for me to remember that when Dan is at work it isn't all fun for him, just because he is with grown-ups all day."

I deeply relate. I find it very difficult not to tally up Doyle's day—a lunch hour spent at Gander Mountain with his fishing buddy from work or possibly at a cool restaurant, his half-hour drive time when he can listen to whatever tunes he wants to on the radio, donut breaks, and so forth—and compare it to my nonstop child-herding day. But when I really think about it, that's just crazy talk. He's under lots of pressure at work, and if he has the occasional fun lunch hour, he richly deserves it.

Another erroneous assumption I make is that he has a tank full of parenting energy after burning up eight hours of computer-programming oomph. *Why is he impatient with a cranky one-year-old after fifteen minutes when I have endured her fussiness for ten hours?* I'll wonder irritably. But I have to remind myself again and again (and then again) that he is just burned out, period, whether by cantankerous computers and demanding clients or a teething toddler. He needs some downtime at the end of the day to recharge his batteries so he can spell me for awhile.

You Need to Get Out by Yourself, and So Does He

"Allowing each partner to carve out a much-needed break is essential," says Dr. Gonsher, a marital and family counselor in Omaha, Nebraska, "so plan for it or you'll start fighting over it."[1] Ya think? Me-time respites here and there are a necessity, not an option. That's why Maggie found a nifty way to make time for, well, Maggie:

> What we have done is found a great day care a few blocks away where Holden goes on Tuesday mornings from 8 a.m. to 12:30 p.m. This allows me to have a set time each week to know I can plan appointments or tackle the cleaning, or many times I look forward to making a good pot of coffee and I curl up on the couch with a book or my latest knitting project. The nice thing is I get Holden all ready and my husband drops him off at day care and picks him up on his way home for lunch . . . this means I can stay in comfy clothes and just chill. I also have a knitting group I go to on Wednesday nights and my husband plays basketball on one night. We also always have a date night (one week we pay a sitter and the following week is usually Grandma). We are still fine-tuning what we do and what our needs are, but I really feel fortunate that my husband sees my need for breaks and is supportive of it.

Maggie feels totally perked up after her weekly break, and I salute her for making it happen. Too many moms feel that even four and a half hours per week of time just for themselves is selfish, but just the opposite is true. Experts say if each of you gets away on his or her own, you'll be more bonded than if you spent every waking second with the little ones. So try to find ways to create these ultra-nourishing pockets of time for yourself, your marriage, and your kids. Like Maggie, you could hire a sitter for a set number of hours per week, or swap evenings with your guy so both of you can get your ya-yas out. Yesterday afternoon, Doyle fished for several hours all by himself. Tomorrow night, I am going out to a local bookstore/coffee shop with my zany bunch of writer pals. We are both getting a vital breather, putting our feet up in our own ways, and restoring ourselves, which is good for our marriage and our kids!

We females seem to clam up when it comes to asserting our need for recuperative time.

You Have Not Because You Ask Not

Hmmm . . . I'm just throwing this out here, but could it be you never get out because you never actually mention that you'd like to get out? For some reason, we females seem to clam up when it comes to asserting our need for recuperative time. "Definitely my hubby gets more free time than I do. But the thing I'm realizing is that it's not necessarily because he demands it, but because I don't let him know when I need/want some time away," Shannon admits. "He is usually more than willing to juggle things or step in to help if I just let him know that I need it."

Again, we seem to believe that our inmost thoughts are somehow transmitting to his mental plasma screen, but that is rarely the case. Sometimes all we have to do is say, "Hey, how about I take this Pilates class at the gym every Thursday night?" Or maybe, if you don't want to spend your time off on such a virtuous activity, "Hey, how about I hit the Krispy Kreme with my girlfriends every Thursday night?"

The point is, tell the man so you can begin implementing a plan to get out. Do you have to spell it out? Yes, of course you do! Did you just get married last week (and find a baby on your doorstep)? He can't read your mind, so be clear about what you want to do and how he can make this happen. "For us, [negotiating time off] has gotten *tons* easier as our daughter has gotten older," says Shannon. "My hubby is more confident that he'll not 'break' our little one, and he's learned what things he and she can do together that they both enjoy. So, if I ask him to take her for a Saturday morning so I can sleep in, run errands, or just spend some time for me, he's not at a loss for things to do (it can help too if I make him a list of things she's currently into for him to choose from). So the biggest thing that has helped us in this area is for me to *communicate* my need for times of refreshment, and then he's shown willingness to help whenever he can."

Plan Ahead

What a concept, yet we so often fail to plan ahead for our outings. Why? Because it can be extremely hard to leave the building when you've got a toddler clamped to your leg like a marine gastropod, and a five-year-old sniveling, "Why do you have to leave me, Mommy?" Of course, the munchkins will be just fine, especially if their capable, nurturing, doting Daddy-O is in charge. (See chapter 3 on maternal gatekeeping if you have a hard time leaving the man of the house to hold down the fort while you play.) If you are hoping for some girlfriend time, and a particular girlfriend also has the marine gastropod situation, this kind of venture requires serious planning indeed. "In trying to coordinate time off with my friends, who are also a very busy bunch of moms, we never seem to get around to agreeing on a time that works for everyone," says Lisa. "So, we usually just end up having dinner together about once every other month." Dinner with the girls every other month? That works for me! Well, it's a start, anyway. Get something on the calendar or you may not leave the premises ever again for purposes of personal frolic time. Or if you prefer some solitary pursuit—bike riding, bookstore/café-ing, Burmese cooking class—plot for those solo excursions as well. Encourage your husband to plan his outings too so everyone is on the same page.

> Get something on the calendar or you may not leave the premises ever again for purposes of personal frolic time.

Sit down with a monthly calendar and map out how many hours you each get to devote to your own pursuits. For example, you could have every other Wednesday evening and Saturday afternoon to focus on yourself, and he could get every other Tuesday evening and Saturday mornings. If some play or sporting event comes up on "your" night or "his" night, swap nights to accommodate each other. With an agenda in place, there's no need to wrangle over downtime, and you'll both look forward to your scheduled time off.

Swap

Matt and Margaret once swapped a four-day cruise (for her and her mom) for a five-day trip to Ireland to hear Celtic music in pubs (for Matt the musician). That's pretty deluxe, but you get the picture. On a smaller scale, we switch out all the time around here. I'll hit *Pride and Prejudice* at the cineplex, swooning with my friend Joy who also loves a movie featuring British men in knickers, and the next afternoon he'll go hunting. I'll spend an evening at a jewelry party and he'll carve out a Saturday morning to fish. George and Emily both love to browse the magazine racks at the bookstore. Now that they have two little ones, they'll take turns, with George flipping through *Details* and Em chasing kids one week, and Em losing herself in a glossy little periodical the next.

Barter with your precious slices of the time pie, and both of you will feel like you are getting what you need.

Tell Each Other to Go Out

"One of the things that's worked well for us is to try to be ultra-supportive when one or the other has an opportunity to go out and do something extracurricular," says Erin. "Both of us try equally hard to say, 'Yes, go do that, clear your head' whenever we can. We each seem to be aware of how tired and hardworking the other is, which somehow makes it easier to be supportive." Erin is so right. When we verbally acknowledge that both parties need to go out regularly, we validate that need and also encourage each other. You start first and say something like, "Hey Babe. You're looking fine as usual but perhaps a little bleached. Why don't you call your best friend Bubba and go fishing this weekend?" He'll think he won the wife lottery!

Go Out with Each Other Too

Factoring your solo time off is only one part of the equation. Much more on this topic later in the book, but obviously you also need to go out together. Or is it obvious? It's essential to your relationship that the two of you regularly step out as a duo. Set aside at least a couple of nights per month where you leave the house together and have fun. Spending time together tearing it up is like a prize for all the hard work it takes to be great parents.

3

I Am Mama, Hear Me Roar

Putting the kibosh on maternal gatekeeping

"Say Da-da," a male voice off-camera urges a baby seen through the lens of a camcorder.

"Ma-ma," gurgles the baby.

"Say Da-da."

"Ma-ma," insists the baby.

A tag line appears at the bottom of the screen: "Baby's first word. Another great reason for being a woman."

This commercial ran in 2000 for the female-oriented Oxygen cable channel, and it triggered some heated posts from offended dads on the Oxygen.com message boards. Were these guys being too touchy? Hmmm. Maybe not, especially if you think about the commercial being part of a bombardment of cultural memos, telling dads they are always going to rank a distant second with their children.

What's more, it looks like women are taking gleeful pleasure in men's second-class status on the domestic front. For a gender reversal, try to imagine a commercial making fun of a woman's helpless attempts to pump gas until a guy comes to the rescue. Yikes![1]

I know moms have a one-of-a-kind role in their children's lives. And somehow, whether we work outside the home or not, we want to run the home show, don't we? There's nothing terrible about this, but we need to be aware that our attitudes toward our husbands and their contributions to parenting and housework may be the very thing that keeps them from pitching in.

Our attitudes toward our husbands and their contributions to parenting and housework may be the very thing that keeps them from pitching in.

Let me just insert an important caveat here. Obviously, some men still regard childcare as "women's work" and affect helplessness to get out of unwanted chores. A young mother I know is pretty much housebound because her husband doesn't want her to leave the place unless the little ones, a three-year-old and a baby, are both sleeping. So don't throw tomatoes at me because you think I am blaming moms entirely for not letting their husbands help out. But in general terms, most guys are willing to offer more domestic support, especially if we are enthusiastic about their efforts.

Some of you are thinking, *If I could only get my husband to help, I would be on cloud nine!*

But seriously now, girlfriends, what happens when the guy does change diapers, supervise the nightly splish-splash, and—*quelle horreur!*—choose an outfit for your little sharp-dressed man or fashionista-in-training?

He does it wrong and it drives you crazy, am I right? Listen to these moms weigh in on how their husbands make them batty when they fill in for a space of time:

> "At what point did eating on the new carpet in one of the kids' rooms sound like a good idea—and did you hear the dryer buzzer going off every five minutes while I was away?"

> "He lets the kids eat candy before dinner (or breakfast for that matter!). They are not made to comb their hair, put on presentable clothes, or wipe their faces when they leave the house!"

> "I figure him just being home is the accomplishment. He watches our son, but if I don't leave him a list of stuff to do, he sits on the couch and watches TV. Even with the list, I get about a 50 percent completion rate."[2]

These are not glowing testimonials, ladies. They are dispatches of despair from women who desperately want and need help from their mates, yet they find themselves pulling their hair out when the help doesn't measure up to their ideals. Who are "they"? Maternal gatekeepers. Mommies who are standing in the doorways of their kids' rooms (metaphorically, you understand), eyeballs wide as they critically survey their husbands' attempts at childcare, ready to whack the poor guy with a diaper bag if he makes one false move.

Well, that would just about describe you, me, and almost every mother on planet earth. We believe, deep down or not so deep down, that we alone can care for our kids in the way they need to be cared for. Even Daddy doesn't do it "right."

So what's the problem? Let's start with the fact that we may be sabotaging our best chance for support in raising our little ones from the very best person to give it: Dad.

"While many mothers . . . believe they need more support in family work, most don't even realize their actions may be placing obstacles in the way. They, themselves, may be limiting the amount of their husbands' involvement,"[3] said Sarah Allen, author of a study on maternal gatekeeping.

Are you Mama Lion at the gate, roaring at Papa Lion to keep away from the cubs only seconds after you asked him to help out more? Do you:

Refold your baby's footie sleepers after your husband already did it?

Make a negative comment about how your husband fed the kids french fries with a side of tater tots for dinner?

Hover while he handles story time one night?

Tell him "We'll give the baby a bath," when what you really mean is "Stand there and hand me something"?

Ask your husband for help with packing your son's preschool backpack and then give explicit directions on what goes inside?

I'm guilty as charged, at least once, for all of the above! This Queen Mama thing is so ingrained, I don't always even know I am doing it. Just recently, I walked behind my family a few paces (much like the crown princess of Japan), and watched as Doyle, holding Phoebe's hand, trotted up the road to Jonah's baseball game. In my mind, I was saying things like, *Don't drag her, for goodness' sake! We are not that late for this game!* and, *Can't you see that she is too little to keep up with you?* Finally, when she did fall on the gravelly pavement, I had to bite my tongue, literally, to keep from berating the man for walking at a clip I deemed inappropriate for holding hands with a toddler.

I work in the basement of our home, a cozy laundry room/basement with wood paneling and innumerous spiders. So when I am working, as I was today, I see my family for little blips of time as I am getting a drink of water or dashing up to the powder room. Well . . . today I have walked by our back deck about three times, trying with all my might not to mention that Doyle should put clothes on Phoebe because she's *one* and it's *October*. Apparently, he didn't think it was vital to clothe the child after stripping her down to a diaper for mac n' cheese at lunch. Fueling my angst is the fact that my neighbor was just joking about a certain celebrity's "white trash" baby who has been photographed wearing a top but no pants, just his Huggies.

Okay, so my neighbor has no kids and she doesn't get it. But I don't want her to think our baby is white trash—whatever that is—running amok on the deck with just her diaper on! Still, I haven't said anything—yet.

Yes, this kind of gatekeeping behavior can be so subtle sometimes, even moms who are very openhanded when it comes to sharing childcare, who are all about equity in parenting, have trouble with this thing.

Check out Ann's first and second emails to me in response to my questions about motherly dominion:

> Email #1: Dan is great with the kids and always has been. If I ever did the maternal gatekeeping thing it was with Adam (our first) and by the time you have a second, well, I was just grateful Dan is a jump-in-and-help kind of Dad. Dan doesn't have to be told what to do or when. He's great about saying, "Don't worry, just go—go out with your friends, or shopping or whatever." Cell phones are also great, because you are always connected and available for any little question and that is a big security for me.

I think my pal's last sentence there was a clue that she isn't always 100 percent able to let her man completely take over. (*Smile.*) But when Ann started thinking about the issue a little more, she was surprised with her discoveries.

> Email #2: Lorilee, in my last message to you I claimed not to do any maternal gatekeeping. Well, in the last week, Dan has caught me red-handed! For things like "Are you pushing Ingrid too high on the swings?" and reminding him endlessly that he is picking Adam up from preschool on Wednesday and what time and what door to go in and . . . you get the idea. So I am guilty, especially when it comes to detail-related items and the kids' schedules.

I had to smirk a little over my friend's admission, because "Are you pushing Ingrid too high on the swings?" could just as easily have been me harping, "Are you walking so swiftly that at any second our tiny, precious child might trip and skin her knee, causing inconvenient bloodshed and buckets of baby tears?"

Dish Panel

Arrrgh! It is so hard to keep a lid on this issue. Listen to Lisa's, Mary's, and Julie's true confessions about their propensity to make themselves Coach Mom while painting Dad as the charmingly inept waterboy.

Lisa: I group the kids' outfits in the closet in chronological order so that he knows what to put on them, when.

Now that my children are older (and a bit heartier!), I trust that he will care for them in a similar manner as I. However, the one thing I still cannot trust him with is dressing the kids so they don't look like little mismatched waifs! On the rare occasions I can escape with some girlfriends overnight to a spa, Toronto, or elsewhere, I group the kids' outfits in the closet in chronological order so that he knows what to put on them, when. (Thankfully they attend a school where uniforms are mandatory, so that helps with the daytime hours!) But as I mentioned before, he really is a rarity in that he is normally as vigilant as I!

Mary: We are the ones with the maternal instinct, so we must know what to do and when, right?

It's easy to fall into the motherly role where you think that as a mother, you are supposed to want to be a mother most of the time and not need to get away. As all mothers know, you think that you are the one person who does *everything* correctly when raising the kids. What we forget is that they are just as much a part of hubby as they are of us. But we are the ones with the maternal instinct, so we must know what to do and when.

Julie: If he would offer to go in and soothe a crying boy, I would quiz him afterwards.

As far as the gatekeeping goes, I know I've been guilty of it, especially when the boys were babies. If he would offer to go in and soothe a crying boy, I would quiz him afterwards: Did you cover him with his white blankie or his blue? How loud is his white noise? Are his socks on under his jammies? Did you take two steps to the right after leaving his crib to make sure the floor didn't creak? Goodness gracious! I sound like the Soup Nazi on *Seinfeld*.

Seriously, it's no wonder the guys don't want to do their share of the childcare sometimes. Why would they want to do something for you when they obviously can't do anything right anyway? Even if Joe Husband is a rocket scientist at work, if he's made to feel like his efforts at home are mediocre—if not downright shabby—the man will surely throw in the towel before folding it the wrong way.

What's up with this inner nag we're harboring, the one who emerges with a critique, a do-over, or instructions so detailed they could be used in data studies at NASA? Basically, we feel like it's mom's way or no way at all, like Kim: "We bond, care for, protect, teach, and love unconditionally like no one else for our children," she said. "I think all mothers to some extent feel that their way is the right way and no one, I mean no one, can compare to them and the way they do things for their children."

Why would they want to do something for you when they obviously can't do anything right anyway?

The issue is further complicated by this fact: Often our feelings of worth and identity are stitched into our domestic and mothering abilities. And because of this, we resist our husband's involvement since it would diminish our value.

Sigh. We are basically confused little Soup Nazis, as Julie described herself earlier, when it comes to maternal gatekeeping. From one moment to the next, we can't decide if it would be better to let the guy make a mistake and take one instead of two steps to the right to avoid the floor creaking—and possibly wake up the baby—or jump in and insist he do things our way.

How ambivalent are we? According to the study done by Sarah Allen, very: "Some women both cherish and resent being the primary care-giver, feel both relieved and displaced with paternal involvement, are both intentional and hesitant about negotiations for more collaborative sharing, and feel guilty and liberated with more involvement from men in family work."[4]

While I agree that Mom pours herself, body and soul, into her children, I do think we need to open ourselves up to the fact that Dad has much to offer that we may not be allowing him to share.

"Generally, men are as involved with their kids as their wives will let them be," says Armin Brott, author of several advice books for fathers and coauthor of the 1999 book *Throwaway Dads: The Myths and Barriers That Keep Men from Being the Fathers They Want to Be.* So why are we moms not opening that gate and letting Dad step through, willing and able to pitch in?[5]

Joanie believes that her and her husband's partner/junior partner dynamic stems from the fact that she's at home with the baby every day. "I'm changing Evan's diapers and feeding him fifty times more often than Don. I've developed my own system and synergy with the baby, and on the weekends, it's almost like Don is messing it all up."

Joanie hit it with this observation. We moms feel we've got the routine down, the system in place, and generally, through trial and error, we've discovered what works with the kids and the housework and what doesn't. And when we see our men on our turf "messing things up" as they try to care for the kids, we can't handle it.

But here's where I've had to pause and say, "Uh oh, I've been a dork yet again." The reason guys mess up is because, well, as Armin Brott says, "[Mom's] not giving him the chance to make the mistakes she's made and go through the learning process."[6]

If a dad is just trying the waters at being a parent and participating in the household, he can feel very clumsy and unanointed. When we're hovering over his every move and barking orders, it's no wonder the guy feels defensive.

The message we send is, "This is the way you do it, and if you can't do it my way, just stand here and look useful."

GIGO

What's the bottom line here? We need to let dads do their thing. If we set ourselves up as the only ones who can feed, bathe, and nurture, guess what? We're the only ones who will feed, bathe, and nurture!

Quit Hogging and Hovering

I remember when my nephew Brenan was a wee baby and I placed him in my dad's arms at a family gathering. Brenan starting fussing, and I think I gave my poor dad about five seconds to calm the kid down before I swooped in and took over. I wince when I think of this, because at the time my dad was healthy and eager to be an Opa. If I'm not mistaken, this was the first time he had ever held his youngest grandson. (When I wrote those words, my dad was in the latter stages of lung cancer. He passed away soon afterward.)

I wish I had let Brenan's Opa, who loved the baby very much, give a credible shot to nurturing and comforting his grandchild. But the truth is, if I hadn't nabbed the kid, my sister-in-law or mom would have.

I once heard a young dad say that if he was holding his son and his son started crying, he had his wife, his mother, his sisters-in-law—i.e., every female within a three-mile radius—standing there ready to grab the kid and stop the wailing. "I'd like to try to soothe Asher myself," he said, "but I don't stand a chance with all that estrogen in my way."

So resist the urge to rescue your baby (and then later on, your older kids). If you just can't stand the sound of your baby's squalling as your partner searches in vain for the perfect soother, bite your tongue and leave the room. If you find that impossible, leave the house altogether and put the ball in his court. If you never relinquish your grip on your little one, your mate will never get the chance to hone his fathering skills. As hard as it may be for you to tear yourself away, let your partner step in while you take a shower, grab a nap, or run a few errands.

The only way for him to learn—just as you have—is with experience. Given some time and space, Dad will get into his own groove.

Also, don't flit around your husband as he attempts to put on a diaper or bandage a scraped knee or run a comb through a tangled snarl of hair. Anxiously peeking over his shoulder every time he tries to accomplish a parenting task sends a big fat memo that you don't trust him to do a good job. So the diaper's on backwards. Who cares? Really, unless he asks for help or a demonstration, leave him to it.

Your Husband Is Not a Clone of You (and That May Be a Good Thing!)

It's only reasonable to assume your husband will do things differently. Accept that there is more than one way to skin a cat (although you probably don't do a lot of cat skinning). "When our daughter was younger I was more of the gatekeeper type and didn't ask for help or welcome my husband's help much," says Shannon. "But as time goes on, I certainly welcome the help and have gotten over the fact that he will do things differently than I do. It's okay. There are numerous ways to put a child to bed at night, while still not deviating far from the normal routines. He doesn't have to read books the same way I do, make meals the same way I do, or even put a diaper on Naomi the same way I do (the backwards look can be fashionable). It's okay. I have to tell myself that over and over sometimes."

Repeat after me (and Shannon): "It's not the end of the world as we know it when our husbands feed the kids cold pizza and popsicles for breakfast." You can fill in the blank. Let the guy do his thing, and maybe you'll even come to learn a thing or two from him. Shannon did: "I realize too that both Daddy and Daughter benefit from the time spent together, regardless of what they are doing (reading, cooking together, etc.). It's bonding time and that's healthy and good."

Look for ways in which Dad excels, and maybe even leaves you in the dust. Erin opened her eyes to the golden qualities in her husband and realized the guy was on to something. "I admit to being really bad at being spontaneous," she said. "I live by the clock and am a terrible playmate. My husband, on the other hand, plays with our daughter beautifully, with reckless disregard for schedules, and she *needs* that time with him, whenever they can get it. It's hard for me not to tap my watch and interrupt them playing basketball or whatever with 'time for a bath' or 'time to do your chores.' I have to work hard sometimes at letting the clock go for this more valuable thing."

And if Dad is doing something you appreciate, say it, out loud! "I try to encourage Mike in the small things he does, since a little encouragement can go a long way in building confidence for him to tackle bigger things," says Shannon. "For example, if I encourage him for spending one hour with Naomi, then it's not such a big jump to ask him to take her out for two hours next week!"

Watch How You Ask for Help

Handing him a checklist of duties and instructions gives the impression that childcare is only your job and responsibility. Instead, ask your man to do his share (more on this sticky wicket in the next chapter on division of labor). If you are the manager—and I admit it's hard not to be when you kinda do run the place—delegating and giving instructions, he will wait for you to ask him for help before jumping in. This ties right into maternal gatekeeping, because if you are running the show and act like the big boss lady, you're standing at the gate and holding it shut. You've got to let him in and let him do things, even if he doesn't do them according to your specifications. This is explored in the next chapter, but for now, focus on letting him share in parenting more fully.

I know that females from time immemorial have expected their husbands to read their minds. You don't want to ask him to change the baby's diaper because, for heaven's sake, can't the man see with his own two working eyeballs that pair of Pampers should have been changed two innings ago? You'd think, but no. (This happened with cave-ladies, who got in snits because their hairy he-men didn't just gather firewood miraculously without being asked.)

Instead, sit down and have a confab about shared responsibilities. It might go a little something like this:

"Larry, love of my life, we need to chat about how you, as our children's wonderful father, can share in the childrearing around here, because between you and me, I might snap like a dry twig at any moment if I don't get to take a load off once in awhile.

"I am sorry for telling you that baby Bono's hair looked like an accidental faux-hawk after you got him ready for church, by the way. I will make a big effort to step back and let you do things in your own adorable, quirky, and sometimes bizarre ways. But we need to work on this."

The olive branch is extended, and the big-picture issues of shared parenting are on the table. You are both helping each other raise a child, after all. Mommy may know best a lot of the time, but that doesn't mean Mommy can't back off and accept the best help the free world has to offer—from Daddy the Great.

4

I'll Do the Dishes and You Wash the Cat

Hammering out a good plan for who does what

Well, well, well. We have come to a very touchy topic indeed: Who does what around the house? How do you and your man divvy up the never-ending amount of childcare and housework that accompany the running of any home? Unless your last name is Trump and your baby's name is Barron, you have grappled with who does what and why. I know Doyle and I have definitely (daily?) wrestled with this. It's one big hot potato. Here's how we hammer out the chores around our house:

The Craker Chore Scorecard

Doyle: Mows the lawn, changes the oil in the cars, vacuums when the babysitter comes over, and once or twice a week clears the deck of dishes, an especially big job since I broke the dishwasher last year (don't ask!). Feeds the dog too, because the dog was his idea and he likes the dog. Cleans up dog poop because, like I said, he is the one who likes the dog enough to clean up her poop.

Biggie: Cares for his offspring while his wife works on books, newspaper articles, or what have you in the basement. This includes changing diapers, feeding people, helping Jonah with homework, and attempting to keep everyone out of the basement so I can have some semblance of a peaceful working environment.

Lorilee: Does everyday stuff like doing dishes throughout the day (although not usually finishing them), picking up toys and string cheese wrappers (or telling the kids to do that, if they are around), tidying the upstairs, bathroom maintenance, laundry, grocery shopping, and "cooking," which usually means that I am responsible for throwing something in a Crock-Pot (thank-you notes to the makers of Crock-Pot liners) or pan (thank-you notes to Tuna Helper), or maybe even a recipe out of *Real Simple* magazine's "Fake It, Don't Make It" column, if I am feeling like undertaking a bold and grand-scale domestic project. (And while we are sending those notes of gratitude, I would be remiss if I didn't mention the lovely rotisserie chicken folks and kind pizza purveyors worldwide.)

Biggie: Cares for offspring the vast majority of the time, and hushes the dog seven hundred times per day when the dog barks at recycling workers, roofers, passersby, squirrels, falling leaves, dust motes, etc.

Yes, that's about how it all shakes out around this casa. How about your house?

Experts say that division of labor is the hottest of hot-button issues among new parents. Though housework may seem like a small issue, it can mushroom into a power struggle that erodes all sweetness in a relationship. Despite the sincerest conversations about chores that precede a wedding, only marriage and children bring out one's true ideals about who does what. Most of the time, tiffs over housework are not about who folds the towels, they're about respect. They're not about when the dishwasher is loaded, they're about caring.

Doing more than your partner can get old—fast. This is especially true when it comes to sharing the childcare load. Parenting is a whole lot more emotionally draining, and sometimes physically exhausting, than shopping or vacuuming or unclogging the toilet. Often we don't give basic oversight of the kids the weight it deserves in terms of true, nitty-gritty work.

For example, let's take a somewhat revolting task such as cleaning the toilet. The commode, you see, won't have a tantrum or start biting its sister or refuse to share its gummy snacks. It won't bawl at high decibels when it scrapes its elbow, because a commode simply does not have an elbow. No, the toilet just sits there quite placidly as you administer bleach and brushing. Unclogging is a different story, but you get my drift, don't you? Well, at least Ann does:

> Because my primary duty during the day is to keep, feed, and supervise two preschoolers, so not much in the way of "chores" is getting done, Dan and I will do a "Kids or Kitchen?" One of us is in charge of the kids and the other

cleans up. Frankly at this point in the day I'm more than happy to tackle a battle with objects.

"A battle with objects"? There's some real truth to that. At the end of the day—filled with beautiful Kodak moments to be sure, but also scraped knees, sibling squabbles, and a toddler fighting her nap with every ounce of her flinty will—I would also rather scrub, fold, or spray some inanimate, soulless tub, towel, or window.

One thing to consider is how we define "work." What drains us the most? Because that's the area where we may need the most efforts from our partner. Don't underestimate the true exertion that comes from parenting. Actually, like Ann articulated, housework is the easy part. The emotional, mental, and physical aspects of childrearing are by far the hardest, most taxing "chore" in our daily lives. You may love being with your kids, but it always takes something from you in terms of energy and heart and soul.

Another foundational matter here is sorting out both sets of expectations about who does what—and how well they do it. Guys, for example, compare their measure of work and skill levels with what their fathers did or do around the house. Or, they might check out that slob Jerry from down the street, whose wife appears to be, as we speak, trimming tree branches about nineteen feet in the air while Jerry relaxes with a beer on the deck.

Compared to Jerry, your man might think, *I'm the Martha Stewart of young fathers*. Well satisfied with his efforts, then, it comes as a rude shock when you're not overjoyed at his haphazard (to you) sweep-up of the kitchen. How do we moms measure our husbands' efforts around the house? Researchers say we measure them against how we ourselves would do the job. If we wipe under the toaster oven and sanitize the counters after every meal, let's say, then his casual swipe at 50 percent of the crumbs will seem like a poor job.

So he's looking at Jerry and thinking, *I am such a huge help, my wife must be overcome with gratitude.* But you're looking under the toaster oven and wondering, *Why is good help so hard to find?*

These things are good to know as we navigate the metaphorical countertops of our lives. Of course, if we do have higher standards in terms of housework, then sometimes we just need to walk away and bite our tongues (see maternal gatekeeping in chapter 3).

Sometimes the shoe is on the other foot, and Hubby has an unrealistic vision of how things should look around his castle. Like Julie's guy. Though he's a helpful partner in many regards, he sometimes doesn't grasp the amount of work she has invested in keeping things running smoothly. "Often, I don't think it occurs to him to ask if I need help," she said. "He thinks things just magically get done."

Or let's take Alvin who, a few months after the birth of their daughter, came home and complained to his wife Liz that the house was a mess—dirty dishes in the sink, baby gear strewn around the living room. "He said, 'This makes me not want to come home sometimes—I can't stand a dirty house,'" recalls Liz, a stay-at-home mom. "Then I said, 'If you don't like it, then you can clean it!'"

Expectations are huge. Alvin expected Liz to clean, and Liz expected Alvin to help out more. Much more about this in GIGO, but the bottom line is that "Duties: Lopsided or Not?" will arise over and over again, especially if the two of you don't open your mouths and present your very personal ideas about housework and childcare.

Dish Panel

Let's listen to my worthy dish panel of moms and find out what goes on behind closed doors in their homes.

Betsy: It's just sort of expected that [the kids] are attached to me in a way.

I do most of the household chores: laundry, dishes, cleaning, cooking, etc. He does the more 'manly' things like taking the trash out, mowing the lawn: the outside work. This is basically because as a stay-at-home mom, I consider a lot of the chores to just be part of my job description. He is very involved when it comes to child-related jobs. Most of his help is on the weekends when he isn't working. But it's kind of expected that when I run somewhere, that I have them with me. If he plans on running to the store for something small, most of the time he just goes by himself. It's just sort of expected that they are attached to me in a way.

Ann: We are just trying to keep our heads above water and get the basics done!

Chores?? We are just trying to keep our heads above water and get the basics done! I primarily do the laundry and the basic housework. Dan does love to cook and I encourage and appreciate his efforts!

Shannon: He is usually more than willing to help if I can just get over my stubbornness in asking for it!

I do more around the house in terms of cleaning, laundry, dishes, and bathing children. My hubby takes out the trash and does other "manly" things (like working on remodeling our spare bedroom). Again, he is usually more than willing to help if I can just get over my stubbornness in asking for it! As far as child-related jobs, my husband hates changing diapers, though he'll do it "if he has to." I often want to throw back the "I've changed over two thousand of these in her lifetime, while you've done maybe a hundred, and you want to whine about it!!!" but I haven't let it slip out yet!

Maggie: I am always shocked by the reality of how much energy it takes to keep up with everything!

My husband is quite helpful and willing to do stuff around the house. He is great about putting Holden to bed (which means lots of book reading!) and also about giving baths. I am so appreciative of this. My issue though is that I still feel all the mental responsibility for everything, like meals, getting groceries, and then actually getting that darn melon cut up before it is overripe. Also, laundry, keeping up on buying diapers, toilet paper, and all of that. My husband does the yard work, shovels snow, takes the dog out, puts dishes away, and pays the bills. I do the rest. I feel my tasks are so ongoing. It isn't just one meal a day, it is three plus snacks. The laundry is constant. It seems like my husband's tasks are more or less one-time-a-week type things, where my tasks are constant. I am always shocked by the reality of how much energy it takes to keep up with everything!

Erin: Honestly, no, he's not as involved as I would like, but I have to guard my heart about that.

Right now, I do more chores, because that's just what makes sense. I work from home and have an established income; he's still getting his business off the ground in an away office, working long hours six days a week. The fact is, he's working hard now in hopes that eventually I won't have to! As long as I don't lose sight of the truth, I can keep better perspective. It's helpful to me that he does want to help and makes some effort. He walks in the door at the end of a long day and says, "What can I do to help you?" I think that's really amazing.

Laura: He is not scared of a diaper, throwing up, or bath time.

Bob and I share the household responsibilities pretty equally. The only thing he doesn't like to do is clean the bathrooms. He voluntarily takes care of the children—he helped create them and verbalizes to folks who ask if he is babysitting that it is called parenting when they are your own, and babysitting when they are a friend's. He is not scared of a diaper, throwing up, or bath time. He is amazingly loving and attentive. God has blessed me with a wonderful, loving husband, as I realize that many husbands believe that it is the wife's job to take care of the house and children.

Jill: Recently, our trade-off of chores looked really smart!

My dear husband changed fewer diapers with each child and now that all three are potty trained I refuse to do any toilet plunging as a balance for poop diapers!

Jamie: He is a great dad, and while he may stiff me sometimes on a dirty diaper, he is very involved in parenting.

At our house, I do most of the "yucky" stuff—mopping, dusting, bathrooms. But my husband does his share. He is not always as helpful as I'd like when it comes to the kid stuff, but he does dress them (if I lay clothes out), changes diapers, and makes sure they eat if I am not around! I get to brag, because my husband is helpful with typical chores. He does dishes, laundry, yard work, and even vacuums sometimes! I have either asked him straight out for help, or when he says, "What can I do?" I give him something specific. I am not picky about how most things are done, but this is why he doesn't do the bathroom—because I'd have to reclean it. Let's face it, most guys' version of clean is not the same as a girl's! I think we do a great job of helping each other with the kids. He is a great dad, and while he may stiff me sometimes on a dirty diaper, he is very involved in parenting.

Lisa: When my friends complain that their husbands have no idea how taxing it can be to be home with a small child all day, I can honestly say mine does!

I really have no room to complain about Dan not shouldering his share of the child-related jobs. Up until Haley was three and a half, I worked part time while Dan was home with her. From three months to three years, Dan changed diapers, fed, bathed, burped, shopped with, cleaned up after, and did everything for our daughter two days a week, ten hours a day. When I quit work after Ryan was born, the bulk of the child-related chores fell to me, but by design. So when my friends complain that their husbands have no idea how taxing it can be to be home with a small child all day, I can honestly say mine does!

Again, the dish from my mom pals out there is a mixed bag, with varying reports of being satisfied—or not—with how the division of labor shakes out at their houses. It's fascinating—to me, anyway—to peek into other people's marriages, be that fly on the wall, and see how folks other than Doyle and myself work it out. Next, in GIGO, we'll explore some ideas for keeping expectations in check and practical ways to get all that stuff done and still be able to talk baby talk at the end of the day (to the dog, anyway).

GIGO

Who's Got the Tougher Job? Don't Even Go There . . .

Stressed couples with overstuffed lives tend to compete over who is working harder, pulling out the balance sheets when they should be pulling out stationery to write thank-you notes. What happens is, you're both fixated on who's right and who's wrong, ignoring how your accusations and scorekeeping are affecting the other person.

Many twosomes grapple with the issue of fairness. We do. And I know I've caught myself making lists of what I have done—kids' school paperwork, bills, banking—stuff that takes work but doesn't translate into a cleaner house or home-cooked meals.

We get caught in a defensive loop—and feel like there's no way out.

Kelly thinks Ryan's job is a piece of cake compared to her mom-on-the-run existence. "It's hard not to think I'm doing more all around, and we do bicker about it," she said. This rivalry, whether it's under the surface or out in the open, destabilizes the haven matrimony is supposed to be. The truth? You're both working your heinies off to keep your family running as well as you do. Prune those antagonistic attitudes that would have you believe you are working harder. Remember, you're not opponents, but teammates working toward the same goals for your little clan.

What Did You Expect? A Cleaning Fairy?

We talked about how men compare their household efforts against their dads and other men, and how we tend to measure their efforts against our own. This is the kind of stuff that needs to get unpacked and out on the table, the sooner the better. There's no time like the present to chat about what you both visualized in terms of who would do what around the joint. Did he expect June Cleaver, without the pearls and pumps, greeting him at the door and beckoning him inside to the wafting aroma of a gourmet meal? Did you daydream about the kind of guy who would maintain your yard so beautifully the local chamber of commerce would call and ask to have your place on a parade of homes?

That's not really happening, unless mac n' cheese with a few hot dog chunks thrown in is his idea of gourmet, and the National Grass Length Committee raises the preferred level per blade to ten inches.

What do you expect? Seriously, take a few moments and think about it. Ask your guy to do the same. Then discuss how realistic each of your expectations is.

"Bob," you might say, "with two kids and a dog, I just can't keep the kind of order you are expecting. But maybe I could step it up in the meal department, especially if you play with the kids while I cook."

And then he might say to you, "Barb, I know a neat yard is important to you, but on weekends I just need to relax. Could we hire that kid with the pierced eyebrows down the street to mow the lawn?"

Take a good, close look at expectations. His upbringing and yours have a lot to do with what you predict will happen around the house. Sometimes this might work in your favor, like my girlfriend whose mother-in-law was a great, nurturing woman but couldn't boil water, bless her heart. Whatever Ann slaps on the table, then, is greeted with enthusiasm by her husband, who can't believe she is such a great cook. "Doesn't take much to surpass Rob's mom," she says, "but hey, I'm going to milk it for all it's worth!" Too bad many of us have the opposite problem, as in MILs who are cookbook authors (I'm winking at my pal Beth L.!) or certified domestic divas.

The point is, talk about what you experienced growing up and how those things shaped, for better or worse, your idea of domestic bliss. You may need to tweak your expectations with a little reality check.

Give Some Tough Love If It's Needed

Okay, you're exhausted and not getting enough assistance in the take-a-load-off department. This is not a man-slamming book, but research does suggest that there are men out there who haven't received the knuckle-dragging-caveman-days-are-over memo. Let your husband know that you have limits. "A well-timed 'your arm's not broken, do it yourself' may occasionally be a helpful reminder that men and women are partners in parenting," says Armin Brott, author of many books on parenting and fatherhood. "One of your biggest challenges may be to close your eyes to the mess and stick to your guns. Your partner will certainly get the message when he runs out of clean underwear. But if he senses that you'll give in before he does, he'll never learn to do his part."[1]

Work It Out

Park the kids at Camp Grandma for an afternoon and hammer out a workable plan for splitting up housework and childcare. What is truly important to each of you? Discuss how you both feel about home-cooked meals versus deli takeout or pizza. Find out your feelings about dusting, cleaning the toilet, making the bed, mowing the lawn, paying bills, and so forth.

Sit down together and make a list of the chores that each of you absolutely hates to do. Doyle would rather have bunion surgery than go grocery shopping, but I actually enjoy it like a little outing. You know, the perky pop tunes on the sound system, the fun little taste tests along the way, the magazine rack . . . some days going to the grocery store is like a visit to the spa! But, *ahem*, as I was saying, if one of you finds a chore horridly unappealing, perhaps the other can handle it with more aplomb.

Make a list of everything that needs to get done. If you're good at laundry or like to do it, it's all yours, baby. Same with his knack for cooking or mopping floors. Look at your list and assign jobs to whoever cares the most about each thing. If he needs the fridge stocked with snacks, he can stock the fridge. If you are picky about how the kids are garbing themselves—and what mom isn't?—then you put together ensembles. Of course, if, say, he could happily step over a toy-strewn living room until the cows come home and holds the same "who cares?" attitude about the rest of the house, it's not fair for you to get stuck doing it just because you care more.

Fairness is your goal, and it takes a lot of love and flexibility to make these negotiations work. Take Maggie, for example, who felt a bit weighed down by the never-ending magnitude of her everyday jobs as compared to what she perceived as her husband's once-a-week tasks. Maybe she could ask her husband to take on one or two everyday tasks such as clearing up after dinner or packing her son's preschool backpack. In exchange, she could possibly tackle weeding the garden or raking leaves in the fall, some typically male sort of job that needs to be done once a week or so.

Your to-do list may not make that much sense to your man.

If your desire to have your daughter's closet cleaned out doesn't make much sense to your husband, try to pose a request this way: "I know it seems weird that I want Chloe's closet clean, but it's important to me that it gets done, especially since your mom is coming to visit and I want her to have some of that closet space. Mostly, I would consider it a very thoughtful thing for you to do for me." Even if he still doesn't get why you need Chloe's closet freed up when your mother-in-law is almost sure not to need that space, he will get the memo that he is being thoughtful by doing this for you. This provides the motivation for getting the task done, even if he wouldn't care if that closet ever got cleaned out. (And let's face it, he doesn't.)

Don't Nag

Trust me on this. Nagging only leads to resentment and it doesn't get the job done any faster. Have a meeting at the beginning of the week to decide who's doing what on the list. Some people even post the list where it can be a good reminder to all involved of the duties to be done. If your husband says he's going to hang those pictures on the wall, and yet the designated wall space is still empty three days later, try to relax. He may be extra busy at work, or be putting it off because he'd rather read a fishing magazine and vegetate. If you're dying for those pictures to be hung, try to let it go for a few more days, at least until your next weekly meeting.

It is also important to be considerate of one another's body clocks. Some folks are morning people and some folks are night owls. Forcing one another to do a project or chore when they really aren't ready to do it only creates tension. Timing is important. At your next discussion, casually mention the pictures to be hung again. Be sweet about it, and use a light touch: "Well, I was going to ask Harold next door to come over and hang those pictures, but I was afraid he would wear those SpongeBob boxer shorts he likes to mow the lawn in. Although I wouldn't mind watching you at work in a pair of those!"

Get Over Yourself, Just a Little

"One thing that's been very important is not to reject his efforts to help me out, however haphazard they may be," says Erin. "He'll do the dishes but won't wash the pots and pans; he'll start the laundry and get the colors mixed with the whites; he'll clean the bathroom and miss grime in the corners. This is okay with me. It has to be okay, because in the end I value his willingness to do what he can more than I value perfection. (I was not always this way.) A colleague of his once complained about trying to do something nice for his wife by cleaning the house; she was so dissatisfied with his efforts that she redid everything herself. The man said, 'Well if that's how she feels, there's no point in both of us doing the same job twice. I won't try that again.' I think he has a point!"

In the end I value his willingness to do what he can more than I value perfection.

Sweet Talk the Guy, Just a Little

At the risk of sounding manipulative, there is a manner of treating someone that encourages them and builds them up, and this treatment also eggs them on to behave more favorably toward you. Do you see where I'm headed with this? Yeah, it's the old "honey attracts flies more than vinegar" thing. So be nice and encourage his efforts. He'll be much more apt to keep plugging away than if you shoot him down, or—don't do this!—redo what he just did. "If I do ask my husband to do something, I'll gush about how much it helped me out afterwards (so that he'll do it again)," said Julie. It's not rocket science, just the age-old concept of how good it feels to hear you've done something well and helped someone out. Tell the man how much you appreciate those beautifully hung pictures and show them off to your friends—within earshot—and the guy will think, *Hey, it pays to be the good guy around here.*

Listen to how Armin Brott describes this phenomenon: "As a group, men generally dislike doing things that make them feel incompetent. At the same time, they're suckers for compliments. So, one of the best ways to get your partner to do something he doesn't like to do is to praise him even when you know you could do it better. Television characters from Lucy Ricardo to Roseanne Conner figured this out long ago, and the same applies in real life: sweet-talk soothes; nagging only irritates. Tell him what a great job he's doing already and ask him to do the same thing again. . . . The more he feels that you're noticing and appreciating his efforts, the more he'll do. Guaranteed."[2]

Pat Each Other on the Back More

You both work hard. And you both need to hear about it. Focus on the way your husband gets up every morning to do his job, or takes out the garbage regularly, or how savvy he was in a recent discipline situation with the kids. It's human nature to react to what's not getting done, but it's far superior to respond enthusiastically to what's going well.

We all crave appreciation and compliments. Studies show our energy levels increase by something like

25 percent when we are praised for the tiniest thing! Celebrate your mutual accomplishment of parenting those spawnlings. Watch for ways to toss him a kudo whenever you can. Cheer each other on as much as possible, because pairs who love well pay each other with admiration and thanks.

So we've investigated our expectations, owned up to our perfectionist ways, and realized the whole household could be running a lot smoother with just a few tweaks in attitude and the way we treat our partner. Hopefully, this all adds up to a richer, truer partnership where the rubber gloves meet the bathroom floor, which is where it really counts.

5

Homicide Is Not
the Answer

How to not murder your in-laws when they have mentioned their potty training theory for the fortieth time

Oy vey! Yes, nothing but the expressive Yiddish language could describe the turmoil that can ensue when Mom and Dad and their moms and dads clash. I have said it before, but truly, Doyle and I are blessed with our parents, with whom we have had few disagreements over the way we raise our kids.

Which is not to say things are perfect. We have all tripped and fallen into that generation gap and lost a tooth or two in the process of figuring out how to co-exist as people of different eras who all love the same munchkins. When Ezra was a newborn, one of our four parents made a comment so politically incorrect it just about made me fall over. And I don't mean "politically incorrect" in a good way! In my postpartum state of wacky hormones and sleeplessness, there was no way I could control my reaction. So I burst into tears, kind of yelled at this dear one with the big mouth to never use that word in my house again, and flew up the stairs in a huge huff.

Can you say "awkward"? Yes, for about two or three months this relative and I tiptoed around one another like people seeking to avoid land mines. Thankfully, in time, the ugly scene melted off the radar and things got back to normal.

So, not perfect in the Craker/Reimer orbit, but not too bad on the whole. At least our relationships with our parents have been heaps better than some of my dish panel and their parents and in-laws. As I sorted through their emails and notes on this topic, some definite themes emerged:

Either Mom or Dad feels stuck in the middle. Like Harvey. His parents have been fault finding of his and Darlene's kids—in front of the kids—and he feels torn between loyalty to his parents and his wife. He agrees with Darlene's view of the situation, but he's worried about losing his tie with his parents. "Darlene is putting a wedge between them and me. I don't like how they handle our kids—my father has made many critical comments. But I have to accept who they are. I realize that I'm not going to change them."

Mom wants her man to stick up for her with his parents, especially when it comes to her mothering methods. Take Stephanie, for example: "I was on my own in trying to fit in with his family because Mark wasn't helping me. His basic attitude was 'just go along with it like I do.' I think it's fair to say he didn't understand his responsibility to protect me and speak up for me in his family. But, in fairness, there were lots of times when I gave up trying to fit in and just rebelled, making it awful for everyone."

Mom spars with Grandma about childrearing methods. Maggie's a good example of this one: "The other day we were over visiting my in-laws and Holden got into meltdown mode because he was tired and in need of a good snack. Now throw in that it was time to leave all the fun toys and attention at Grandma's and he starts whining. Grandma grabs his arm firmly and starts to tell him how he should behave. (My feelings at this moment are to handle this with understanding as he is tired and hungry and is sad as it is time to go. . . .) Here is where the problem for me comes in. . . . I long for my husband to tell his mom nicely, 'Mom, we will handle Holden' and then grab our son and get in action. Instead, she does her thing, I am standing there wanting to have my husband lead and wanting to protect my child from possible shame-based grandparenting, and ultimately end up stepping in to take care of Holden and feeling like everyone thinks I am a big jerk, and like I don't let my husband lead!"

Mom has a storybook ideal of her relationship with her kids' grandparents. When Darlene got pregnant, she thought it would pull her closer to her husband's parents. But she still felt like an outsider. "I've always wanted to feel I'm as close to my mother-in-law as her own daughters are," says Darlene. "But his mom—and dad—seem increasingly impatient with the kids and with me."

Talk about one loaded hot potato! Getting along well with the oldsters seems to be a dying art form for so many in our generation. Many moms did rave about their parents and in-laws, so don't think everyone was down on the Buick generation. Some moms declared their love for their husband's parents, yet with a few caveats, such as Maggie (above) whose in-laws are much older (77 and 80) and therefore that much more out of sync with the "new" parenting styles. Really, the responses to this topic ranged from blathering adoration of Granny and Gramps, to chafing here and there, to utterly horrible messes that would take a miracle to clean up.

I don't want this chapter to be problem-heavy, so just to let you know, I do give some positive solutions in the GIGO section, as always. But I believe that in hearing other people's stories of their relationships with their parents and their husband's parents, you will be better able to get a handle on your own oldster troubles.

Dish Panel

When in-law problems exist, it just plain messes up your marriage. In fact, generational clashes are one of the biggest reasons couples seek marriage therapy.

"Young marrieds often face in-law friction, because families tend to have different personality dynamics or ways of doing things," says Jane Greer, PhD, author of *Gridlock: Finding the Courage to Move On in Love, Work, and Life*. "What compounds . . . the problem is that [Mom and Dad] aren't on the same wavelength about how to deal with it, and this disconnect is unhealthy for their relationship."[1]

Give a listen, then, to my dish pals as they yammer a bit about how they handle that hot potato. Some burn their fingers regularly, while others have found a way to cool things down.

Unwanted Advice

Whew! As Geoff Williams tells us in an article in *Baby-Talk*, when the precious grandbabies come along, some folks turn into GrandZillas . . .

My parents' unceasing advice makes me feel like a little boy again.

In the earliest of our first baby Isabelle's days, we would have the same conversation every visit: "She must be freezing. You're letting her wear that?" my mom would ask. "No, of course not," I'd stammer, looking down at our three-month-old. "Your real granddaughter is in the car, dressed much, much warmer. Oh my, whose baby is this?"

Actually, I wish I could think that fast on my feet. Usually, I just stammer something incoherent as my dad runs to turn up the thermostat and my mom hands me a newspaper clipping about a baby who recently developed frostbite because her father was carting her around in too few layers.[2]

When Geoff said his mom made him feel "like a little boy again," he hit on a big issue. I think that when a guy feels like a little boy, he won't stick up for himself—or his wife—in any number of sticky situations. That is definitely something to watch for in your husband and in yourself. Do your parents make you feel like you're not exactly a competent, grown-up wife and mother?

Like probably everyone on the planet, we still like to please our parents.

Comments about Money

Old habits die hard. Like probably everyone on the planet, we still like to please our parents. Ray Romano made a fortune from a sitcom based on this subject. Little zingers about cash or lack of it can really, well, zing!

Says Janae, "In the first five minutes of any visit, my in-laws will manage to push at least one big financial button. Comments such as, 'The house is so much smaller than it looked in the photo, especially given what you paid,' makes me nuts. Ten minutes later, my husband and I are both irritated at each other because of what his parents said!"

Becky: The issue we have is that my parents seem to base success only on financial gain.

They always seem so disappointed in us that we don't have a nice house, can't buy the kids whatever they want, can't just get a babysitter whenever we want and go out, etc. No matter how old you get, you always want your parents' approval, and it is hard emotionally when you feel like you are doing what is right for your family, but you don't get their approval for the choice you have made.

Grandparenting Style

Becky: Our kids are too much for our parents to handle.

We had kids late in life. Our parents aren't as young as most grandparents and just can't handle our kids well. The kids are just too much for them it seems. My parents will only babysit one child at a time and my MIL just lets them run wild and do whatever they want when she watches them because she is too tired (or lazy?) to set limits and really "watch" them.

Catharine: My child has never spent even a minute alone with my mother-in-law.

My MIL really pushed to have grandkids, so you would think that she would be great when the grandkids come around, right? Not really. She has gone above and beyond letting kids get away with stuff just because she is the grandma to the point of dangerous—like the time she tried to feed our nephew Diet Coke out of the can at six months old, or the time she fed him chocolate pudding at three months old, or the time she let him stick his finger in an outlet at one year old because she wouldn't childproof her house, or the time she gave her granddaughter a chip at nine months old and stood by while she choked wondering why there was a problem! Like I said, the list goes on and on, which is why my child has never spent even a minute alone with her! Perhaps it's even harder for me to let my child be around her because I know that my mother, who died soon after our baby was born, would have been such a wonderful grandma to him.

The main problem with Catharine's MIL being such a bad granny is that she's the mother of her husband, just to point out the obvious. This means Catharine must deal with this woman, and even try to love her, for the sake of her marriage. Sounds like that would be hard to do!

Meg: I have great in-laws—they would do anything for us. The issue is really more generational.

They think parenting should be handled like it was when they were raising kids. So we have different parenting styles and they don't seem open to accepting the new ways, even if I preface stuff by saying, "Well, our pediatrician says . . ." My mom-in-law feels a need to get on Holden if we are out to eat or anywhere, like she feels like she is the parent. She also reminds us that her kids never did any of the typical kid things, like fits in the grocery store, throwing food off the high chair, etc. They were always perfect in her mind!

If Meg complains about her in-laws, she may have a defensive hubby on her hands. Who wants to have their parents criticized, even by their spouse? This is why it's so important to frame any comments to the man with the utmost tact—always easier said than done!

Julie: We've given them many opportunities to babysit (which she says she wants to do), but they are always busy.

Ah, the in-laws . . . No, mine are pretty good. They love and adore our boys to death. I probably only have little personality conflicts that I hope I keep hidden! My in-laws are very social people and have a wide circle of friends that keep them busy. They also travel a lot. My MIL will sometimes complain that she doesn't see the kids enough. We've given them many opportunities to babysit (which she says she wants to do), but they are always busy. So if a week has gone by and she hasn't seen the guys, they will stop by on a Sunday afternoon (unannounced) and play with our kids. I just wish they would ask when a convenient time would be instead of coming during nap time or dinner.

If Julie's husband is more open to having his parents drop in—and he just might be, they're his folks, after all—she's got a bigger fish to fry than her own annoyance: a man who doesn't get why she doesn't welcome his parents. This just adds another layer of complication to what might be the simple issue of setting visiting boundaries for the in-laws. Ahh, the many complexities of the in-law relationship!

K: We both feel my husband's mother does not try to put forth enough effort to see her grandchildren, and it causes great stress when we are together.

We have three sets of grandparents, two of which live over ten hours away, and yet they see the grandkids much more than his mom who is only two hours away. To say that doesn't go over well would be an understatement!

Leave and Cleave?

When I hear horror stories like Melinda's, I resolve right then and there to try my utmost to be flexible someday when it comes to my own kids' mates and their holiday customs. I mean, I can see why certain matriarchs get their shorts in a knot about newcomers wanting to do things according to the traditions set forth amongst their own kinfolk. It's got to shake them up to suddenly have to accommodate so-and-so's notions about how many presents under the tree, turkey or ham, and football game on or off. Truly, it's amazing how ingrained and beloved these rituals are and how much they mean, especially when "threatened" by interlopers who happen to love the same people. Read on, and you'll see why I feel deep empathy for Mel and her unbending MIL situation.

Melinda: We've been married nine years now and we still have yet to develop our own family traditions.

My MIL adores her son and her two granddaughters. But she is stuck in this tradition warp. We've been married nine years now and we still have yet to develop our own family traditions. Before I entered this state of wedded bliss, I loved holidays almost as much as men love the Super Bowl. Now I loathe them. I see dates creeping up on the calendar and the tummy aches start and the pimples emerge. Although progress has been made, my husband hasn't really mastered standing up for his immediate family. That leave and cleave thing never really happened. Once entangled in those apron strings, you're left to be hung. Tragic indeed. But there's always the dream that someday . . .

You've heard the ladies—and one guy—gripe about what gets under their skin as far as their relationship with their parents and in-laws. But the big fat question is really, How do these irritants affect the way you love and interact with each other? Because therein lies the rub, if you know what I'm saying. These are the quandaries that can drive a wedge and a half between you and your main man.

Maggie: I feel mad that my husband doesn't see how important this is to me . . . that he stands up for us and lets his parents know we are in charge of our family.

Often I am mad all the way home from seeing my husband's parents because of the position I am put in over there, defenseless against their way of undermining our parenting. I really wish Karl would tell his mom we will handle Holden and his behavior issues. I would have peace of mind, respect for my husband in a new way, and would just feel more relaxed. Instead, I feel super *on duty* all the time, and like I am the only one who feels the pressure of responsibility. I also feel mad that my husband doesn't see how important this is for our family and for me, that he stands up for us and lets them know that we are in charge of our family.

Get Out Your Spare Tire Kits, Ladies

Ach! What a heavy slog this getting along with kin thing can be! My dish panel have been forthright—sometimes achingly so—in regards to relational pitfalls that have tripped them up and caused them to feel a range of emotions—from trifling irritation to frustration to quasi homicidal—toward the older generation. I do believe that many families do get along quite famously, with minute issues if any at all. Like Tenny, below, we are blessed when we have a close relationship with our parents, and even more enriched when we have "bonus" parents to love and be loved by. Because as we've heard from these moms (and one dad), when that wheel comes loose on the family bus, your marriage could be headed for a breakdown.

Just below are some tire-patching/pumping/replacing tips, if you'll indulge me the extended metaphor. You can mend the highly charged rifts in these key relationships. It won't be easy, but it will be worth every bitten lip, turned cheek, and awkward moment you endure to make things better.

But before we get to the solutions, here's a fresh voice from someone who genuinely adores her in-laws, just to refresh your reading palate before we roll up our sleeves and get down to the nitty-gritty. Call me Pollyanna—you wouldn't be the first—but it's always good to end on a high note.

Tenny: I would love to see my in-laws more!

My husband is more of the cleave-and-leave type. But he is recognizing more and more that his parents' healthy marriage is great for us to see and for our kids to see. I just love being around his parents because I came from a broken but loving home. Seeing two people (parents) who still love each other so much is something I didn't realize that I missed, but I did.

GIGO

First, Patch Things Up as Best You Can

Remember my blowup at the politically incorrect relative? These stormy moments can and do happen. Darlene and Harvey, for example, flew out his parents' door mid-visit, enraged that Harvey's dad was once again insulting their child in front of them. It felt right in the moment, as they were filled with protectiveness and righteous indignation over the FIL's jabs, and they can hardly be blamed for getting upset. But when they cooled down, they realized that patching things up would be an *extremely* awkward and uncomfortable endeavor. What to do? Never having contact again was tempting, yet not realistic. The reason family fights are so awful and painful is because it's family—those people who changed your diapers, bought you school supplies, and fed you for at least eighteen years. If a friendship gets toxic, it's a whole lot easier to give a pal-turned-foe the heave-ho. No, it was a must for Darlene and Harvey to reconcile with his parents, and of course the burden lay on them to make that first excruciating move.

Experts say that walking away is sometimes the only way to prevent something even worse—words flung out in anger. But when you walk out that door, the bridge, if it's not burned to a crisp, is definitely charred in spots. Those steps walking back will be some of the most uncomfortable ever. Hot coals come to mind, not to mention broken glass.

That's why you need to be armed with a plan, a set of new and improved ground rules for the future relationship you're trying to build with your parents or in-laws.

Present a United Front

So many moms have told me they feel unprotected by their husbands in terms of how his family treats them. They long for their husbands to stick up for them and their mothering. Why do some husbands have such a hard time defending their wives and themselves to their parents? Why is leaving and cleaving so difficult? I wish I knew. Every family is different, though, and you have to remember that these patterns and ways of working things out are fundamentally hardwired in your husband's very soul. You are looking at the situation with much more objectivity, even though you may feel anything but objective.

You think, *What's the big whoop about Jason telling his parents, "Hey, could ya back off a little on the potty training? Our doctor says two and a half is well within the normal range of being trained. Little Ava is just simply not ready, and this is how my wife and I have decided, as her parents, to handle it."* Instead, Jason—CPA, hockey coach, church deacon—appears to become shy, ineffectual, and unable to speak at all when his parents start in about how terrible it is that their granddaughter is still evacuating her bowels in a diaper. It makes you want to scream.

Give the guy a little slack here. He may be thinking that if he said anything it would sound disrespectful to his parents. In his family, perhaps, people don't challenge the folks much, even though the kids are in their thirties now. He's following that unconscious script we all follow when it comes to our parents.

Your guy needs to know how this makes you feel. You need to sit down, when you feel calm and relaxed, and say that you need the two of you to be a united front when it comes to his parents. (Of course, it's vice versa if you are the one with parent issues.) Tell him you want to respect him more and feel closer to him, and that forming a more cohesive couplehood when it comes to his family would do just that.

Doyle would rather subject himself to a makeover on cable TV than confront someone in his family about something. Yet, once in a great while, it needs to be done.

Ugh. Ick. Deep sigh. It ain't gonna be pretty, so make sure you tell your man you know that. But the rewards will be fantastic when the two of you are on the same page. After you make a plan (see below) to troubleshoot your specific problem areas (sounds like I'm talking about thighs here, doesn't it?), have a powwow about how to present a united front.

The Amalgamated Arnsteins

Go to the oldsters together and speak in "we" and "our" statements: "We felt bad the last time we saw you and wound up walking out. We want to talk with you about it and make sure it doesn't happen again to us." The more solid you are as a couple, the more prepared you'll be to handle any zingers that fly your way.

You want your man to be your knight in shining armor and leap to your rescue, right? Don't we all? Tell him how much admiration would radiate from your being if he found a way to calmly yet firmly defend you and his family with talk like this:

"When you talk to our daughter about potty training like that, we find it upsetting."

"It's important to us that you focus on what our kids do right."

"We know you have a different viewpoint on (potty training/sugar/tantrums/fill-in-the-blank), and you are definitely entitled to it, but we are going a different way on this one. There's not just one right way to view this issue. We are Gigi's parents, and we need your support as much as possible."

Listen, the prize at the end of this difficult speech—or series of speeches, possibly—is that the grandparents won't be able to divide and conquer you two if you present a joint face. You'll be closer, more in tune with each other, and subsequently deeper in love than before you confronted this obstacle together.

Make a Plan, Stan

If, like Melinda's unyielding MIL, you face the same dilemma over and over with the grandparents, it's time to sit down and hatch a plot. So, every Thanksgiving there is big tension over where you spend the day? (I'm always amazed that so many MILs have apparently never grasped the concept of taking turns!) Resolve that two months before the holiday, you tranquilly announce (via email if you absolutely must) that this year you will be spending Turkey Day with the other side of the clan. Or you have decided as a family to serve at the soup kitchen this year—it's always hard to argue with a humanitarian pursuit—or whatever it is you've planned to do with the day. "We'll miss your sage stuffing, Ma, but maybe you can wrap some up for us? Otherwise, we'll just have to wait until next year."

Make up your mind that any sputtering that comes from Camp MIL will be greeted with kind yet firm re-iteration of your plans. "Yes, Mother Hermantrude, I do understand that you're upset about us missing this

Thanksgiving, but we've made our decision and we're sticking to it."

She'll live, and she may even adjust her notion of how malleable you two are. Set limits together. If your parents drop in unannounced every Sunday afternoon, hammer out some boundaries to keep the relationship from getting tense and resentful.

"Hey, you guys are great grandparents, and we appreciate you so much, but we are finding that Sunday afternoon is not the best time for you guys to drop in. Would Saturday evenings work for you? Or why don't we connect early in the week and figure out a good time for a visit? That way we won't be asleep or whatever, and we may even have some food in the house for snacks!"

The key is, come up with a plan, set limits you both agree on, stick to them, and remember, you and your husband have more power in this relationship than you think. Sticking together will only improve your relationship with your parents and in-laws, not to mention infuse your own wedded bliss with new strength and intimacy.

Before you get relegated to the kiddie table next Thanksgiving, use some savvy when it comes to accepting advice from your parents and your guy's parents.

Your parents and in-laws probably have ironclad notions about how kids should be raised. Like Maggie's in-laws, who believe children should basically be seen and not heard. Maggie could easily get her undies in a bunch—who wouldn't?—next time her MIL acts mortified at little Holden's tantrum at a restaurant or an outing. "We never allowed my children to act like little savages, especially not out in public."

Thirty years ago, people just didn't take their kids out to restaurants nearly as much as we do these days, but it probably wouldn't be helpful to point that out. Usually it does help to say, "Our pediatrician says . . . ," but Maggie's MIL is apparently a tough nut to crack. Sometimes all you can do is soothe your child the best you can, murmuring a short explanation of why he is having a meltdown.

"He just loves playing at your house so much, it's hard for him to process that it's time to go." Or,

"He missed his nap, so we better get going so he can fuel up."

Email Granny an article about tantrums from a reputable magazine or website. Maybe if she reads the info from an objective source, she'll lay off you.

There will be occasions when the older generation simply will not grasp or respect why we do the things we do or allow the behavior we do. My dad used to get edgy when we allowed Jonah and Ezra, as toddlers, to make towers out of jam packages and creamers at a restaurant table. *What else are they supposed to do?* I would think. The activity sheet the waitress gave us was not going to cut it for a two-year-old.

There's much less of an expectation now that a two-year-old can sit still for thirty minutes, waiting for his food. Our generation, by and large, believes that kids will be kids, and though that doesn't give them a license for

There will be occasions when the older generation simply will not grasp or respect why we do the things we do or allow the behavior we do.

flinging ketchupy fries at passersby, we have to take into account their capacity to function well if they are tired, hungry, or otherwise unhinged.

Here's the core issue: Our parents want to see their grandchildren shine, because in a very real way, our kids' behavior reflects on *their* job as parents to us.

I would suggest that if the oldsters truly cannot handle a potential meltdown or display of incontrovertible toddlerhood at a public place, then do avoid public outings at all costs, at least until your child can be expected to handle these outings with more maturity. Why ask for friction?

Rethink Your Expectations

Almost everyone enters marriage with some wishful thinking about making close connections with their in-laws. Let's face it, we want our relationship with our in-laws to be one big fat slobbering love fest. We picture a loving grandmother for our children, happily splashing in puddles with her little cherubs, and instead we may get a Cleaning Nazi who has a cow when her grandson gets mud on her veranda.

Darlene fully expected Harvey's family to embrace her unconditionally. Darlene also assumed that Harvey's parents would be head over heels in love with their grandchildren, mirroring the close relationship she's always enjoyed with her own grandparents. Instead, she has her father-in-law making snide comments about how chubby her daughter is, or how uncoordinated her son is.

The bubble burst a long time ago as far as Darlene's expectations of her in-laws, but a part of her still kind of holds on to the image of sweet, doting Granny and Gramps who think her kids hung the moon. Instead of clinging to this fairy tale—and wishing for a relationship she doesn't have—it's time for Darlene to get real.

Recognize who your in-laws or parents really are. If an oldster is negative, accept that you can't change his behavior. But what you can do is change your reaction to his behavior.

Defuse Negative Comments

What's worse than a grandparent who is full of jabs, maybe not about your parenting, but about your kids? *Yeee-ouch!* And it's not exactly like we moms are thick-skinned when it comes to our precious, darling, beloved offspring. How do we handle the little—or big—zingers that fly out of some oldsters' mouths?

Try turning a critical comment inside out. Here's what I mean: If, say, you pick up your baby when she starts crying and your FIL says, "Oh, we're spoiled, are we?" you could say, "Well, actually, she's not spoiled, she's a baby. My doctor says it's impossible to spoil a baby this small. They need all the love and nurturing they can get at this age."

Say this nicely and maybe with a smile if you can stretch your lips that far. Don't mention the fact that this same relative talks baby talk to his dog, microwaves dog treats to the perfect temperature, and lets the mutt share a pillow with him. Don't mention it out loud, or right then, I mean.

Or . . .

Grandparent: "Baxter should act his age."

You: "He's three. He is acting his age." (Lips curved upwards, once again.)

Grandparent: "Wiley is so strong willed and rough all the time."

You: "Wiley's a rough-and-tumble kid, that's for sure. But the silver lining is that he doesn't cry when he falls down, and he really takes life in stride. We think he'll make a great leader someday if we channel his qualities properly, not to mention a stellar linebacker!"

Grandparent: "Lulu is so clingy all the time! Why is she so insecure?"

You: "Actually, I asked my doctor about Lulu's clinginess, and he said some kids are just naturally more reserved and tentative. The flip side is, she's always so kind to other kids in preschool. She really has a gentle, sensitive spirit."

You can see where I'm going with this. It's so easy to become defensive when a parent or in-law is criticizing your child, but try hard to take it easy. Comebacks can have humor—a little joke always smooths things out— but make sure they are delivered gently and without accusation. The content of the message—that you are

proud of your children and will always defend them—
will be heard if it's delivered without hostility.

Get Out of That Rut

Crack your mind open, just a little, when it comes to
your stickiest relationship. Maybe your MIL has a good
potty training tip that you could try. Hey, maybe she
knows how to apply plant CPR to that bromeliad you've
been killing in the corner of your house. Be open to
whatever little bridges are out there for you to cross.

Like my pal Troy, who happens to be a shrink, always
says, "Baby steps, Lorilee, baby steps." (He's not *my* shrink,
mind you, but that's just the way he always talks.)

Just to toss out another cliché, the bumps are what
you climb on. Above all, learn to not take these things
so deathly personally. When parents are overly involved
in their adult child's life, it's usually a result of their own
emotional neediness, not of something you did or didn't
do. Hopefully this thought can give you and your man
the strength to forge together, crack those relationship
puzzles, and be the mom and dad your kids need you to
be. After all, you're not raising your kids to please your
parents or your in-laws. Focus on your marriage relationship above all else, and all the other pieces should
fall into place.

6

Dad's a Homebody and Mom's a Social Animal, or Vice Versa

How an extrovert and an introvert can mesh their social styles

Differing social styles can drain the fun out of any relationship. Throw munchkins into the mix and you've got an even bigger social style stalemate. "Mark would rather sit in a closet than go out and socialize on weekends," says Krista. I can deeply relate to this scenario.

Doyle and I are as opposite as a mug of black diner coffee and a cinnamon Frangelico soy latte with low-fat whipped cream and Dutch cocoa shavings. Plain married Fancy—that's what happened with us, and that's what happens just about every time the parson pronounces you Mr. and Mrs. Opposites Attract, and then when it comes to their social life as a couple, they need to figure out how to mesh those different ways of unwinding.

In your marriage, you may be the homebody who thrives on quiet and solitude, and your husband may be like Fun Bobby on *Friends*. Or you could be the Pink in the relationship, always wanting to "get this party started."

That's me, Pink, but with a less ferocious sneer and much less of a mohawk. I am wired to par-tay, and I just groove on people—new ones, old ones, you get the idea. Oh, I have my moments when I need peace and alone time, but often, especially when it comes to the weekend, I am ready for some turbo socializing.

Doyle has a degree in pastoral studies, but I always tell folks my man just doesn't like people enough to be a pastor. Like, for instance, if he was a pastor and someone had a crisis between November 15 and December 1—firearms deer hunting season—he would respond like this: "Hey man, what do you mean your marriage is falling apart? Could ya keep it together until December 2?"

Doyle's weave is such that he simply doesn't want or need much in the way of camaraderie with human beings. Squirrels? Trees? Babbling brooks? Those are his "peeps" and they're not even human.

Tenny can relate. "My husband is very antisocial and I can start a conversation with anyone," she says. "We knew this when we got married and *neither has tried to change it about the other person* [italics mine, because the girl's on to something!]. I have become more of a homebody and just enjoy being with my husband and kids at home (living in the woods will do that to you). But in situations like church, we both know that I need a kick in the pants to get going while he's been at the door for fifteen minutes."

Tenny, sister, we were separated at birth. Come Sunday morning, I am like a pioneer woman who hasn't seen a warm body except her own kin for a week. Has Doyle ever waited fifteen minutes for me to quit jibber-jabbering with everyone and their uncles? Has Doyle ever waited *less* than fifteen minutes?

So I like to catch up with friends. Is that so wrong?

Some couples are the opposite. Julie and her man, for example, have gone ten rounds over his Fun Bobby schtick and her more reserved, orderly personality. "Brent is definitely more outgoing than I am," she says. "He finds someone he knows anywhere we go. Our biggest issue is that I am a planner, and he would just as soon live without a clock. He is always running late for meetings, church, coming home from work. . . . He will say he'll be ready to leave in ten minutes, then proceeds to take a fifteen-minute shower, look for clothes, decide to clean his eyeglasses, need to search for paperwork to take with. He was late for pictures for our own wedding, so I knew it was coming!"

(Hint: Julie, Brent was probably late for your wedding pics because he ran into someone he knew from elementary school on the way to the shoot. They got talking and he lost track of time. Why? Because for us social animals, talking and connecting are always more important than the trivial little details in life, such as wedding photographs!)

Reverse relational styles are so common, it's a marvel anyone similar ever gets hitched. Fun Bobby and Pink almost never get married, because then who would pay the bills?

Nope, God knew Doyle needed someone to drag him to birthday parties and potlucks, and that I needed a guy who would teach me that life isn't just one big social gathering. We are together, in part, to expand one another's borders, get each other out of our comfort zones, and do things and experience things that go beyond what feels natural and safe. It's called growth: expansion, development, progress!

But how do social opposites hammer out a plan so Pink gets her ya-yas out and her husband (Brown?) gets the peace and quiet he needs?

Underscoring all of this is the fact that when we have kids, our differing social styles and the problems that crop up because of them are just magnified. It's ironic that, just at the stage of life where we need the most rejuvenation—either through solitude or socializing—we have two or three short people who, by their very nature as children, constantly demand that we don't get it. The negotiation process, then, is far more complicated than ever in terms of two social opposites getting what they need. The time-off pie we talked about in chapter 2 is sliced more thinly with every child, and not only do we have to bargain far more for a chunk of freedom (i.e., grown-up pursuits), we also have to collaborate in a much more sophisticated manner on how the extrovert and the introvert can both get what they need.

Often, Mom and Dad fight over making plans, get frustrated, and end up going off to do their own things all the time. It's tempting. But the richer, more rewarding plan involves some savvy adaptations, a dose of respect and compassion, and a pinch of creativity. Like Krista, we can learn to work out our differences for a stronger, closer union. The first step might be to walk a mile in his size 11's to get a better grasp on what makes him tick.

"When we went to see a counselor, I found out that when I make Mike socialize so much when he's not in the mood, it's akin to him asking me to sit in a dark closet for two hours," she said. "That was really key in helping us understand each other's social styles and work at compromise."

Here's another thing to keep in mind: Don't be thinking your social stalemate will improve when the kids are in school, or your schedules are more in sync, or fill in the blank with your own excuse. Don't just wait for things to get better. Experts say dyed-in-the-wool traits such as personality and preferences don't change all that much over time.

But if you settle on a great plan for both your social styles (more in GIGO), you'll come out stronger and more gaga for each other in the end. This way, no one has to party themselves silly *or* sit in a closet for hours—unless of course that's what they want.

Dish Panel

How do you deal with your different social styles? When I uncorked this question, my dish panel spilled in a big way.

Lisa: Once we had kids, I became much more of a homebody.

When we started dating in college, both Dan and I were very social—we loved attending parties with friends, having people over once we were married, and going out with friends to dinner, on weekend vacations, etc. However, once we had kids, I became much more of a homebody. Dan would like to entertain and go out more than we do, but with his weird work schedule, we're not always "primed to party." Also, my son was never happy with a babysitter other than my mom or grandma, so if they weren't available, I was happy to not go, whereas Dan would've happily hired some teenage girl off the street to watch the kids. But again, as they get older and we're out of that "baby stage," we are doing more with friends from church and their families, which always ends up being a riot!

Tenny: My in-laws love that my husband married a Chatty Cathy!

One plus to our "opposites attract" marriage is that my in-laws and sister-in-law love that my husband married a Chatty Cathy. They actually get to know what's going on in his life in the present, and not just two years after the fact. I've always been one to keep in contact with people, so it suits my husband's friends as well."

Is TV Coming between You and Your Guy?

Do you end arguments with your guy by threatening to vote him off the island?
Have you used words like "hematoma" to describe swelling and bruises?
When you think about building a new house, does a part of you believe it could actually happen in a week?

If you answered yes to any of these questions, you may very well be a sofa spud, not that there's anything wrong with that. I write tons about TV in my moonlighting job as an entertainment reporter, and I believe it's the number one arbiter of our culture. But that's another book altogether. What does tube watching have to do with your varying social styles? Lots, if one of you likes to hunker down and watch more than the other.

Many couples like to relax and tune in together, especially when the little ones have been tucked in for the night. But for some, one or the other wants to throw that console/box/screen out the window. Listen to Janie spill about how TV has taken over her marriage:

"I'm starved for adult conversation, but Byron doesn't hear one word I say," she said. "He is a wonderful, hands-on father, though I hate when I come home from someplace and the kids are all sitting there with him, watching sports all the time. I feel like they won't feel valued if all the attention he gives them is when the commercials are on. Recently one of my sisters asked if he still watched sports as much as he used to. Byron said he'd gotten better. Excuse me? He can discuss baseball plays from twenty years ago, but he can't remember what I said ten minutes ago. That's not cool."

No, not cool at all. Thankfully, Doyle doesn't watch sports too often—I actually am the sports watcher in the family with my

---

hockey addiction—but he does tune in to hunting and fishing shows quite often, which make my eyes glaze over.

Recently we were at a couple's house for dinner, and while the kids were situated at the main table, the four grown-ups were seated on the couch with TV trays. The guy, a huge hunter, popped in a moose hunting DVD while we ate. He and Doyle were transfixed by the camo drama unfolding before them, while my girlfriend and I made awkward conversation around the lovely noises of mammal carnage coming from the TV.

I could tell with one glance at Moose Man's woman that this move was highly uncouth in her mind. Yup, I gave him ten seconds after we left that night to receive a gutting of his own. When I told Doyle that his buddy was dead moose meat, he was oblivious. "Really? Huh. I didn't notice anything like that at all." Big surprise.

Obviously, Mom and Dad are not always on the same page when it comes to the tube. Like Janie, sometimes the TV can isolate a once cozy twosome. How can TV Tom and his lady cross the distance between them on that couch, stop sniping, and start snuggling once again? First, if man decompresses in his Barcalounger after a hard day's work, we may have to learn to accept his choice of hobby and try to be more understanding about the fact that our guy finds relaxation in losing himself in the game (or *CSI*, or whatever). It's not going to be very helpful to tell the guy he has a lame hobby either. Trust me, off-the-couch leisure pursuits can be just as bad or worse in terms of causing a disconnect!

If you constantly throw zingers at the guy for his viewing habits, he'll feel shamed, like you're his mommy, and *ooh, ick*, who wants that? Instead, when you feel somewhat serene about the whole thing, sit the dude down—not in front of the you-know-what—and get in his face about how horrible he's being to you. (Okay, you know that ain't so. I just wanted to make sure you were paying attention.) Seriously, it's time for a confab, but make it a constructive one with this kind of talk:

"Bill, I love you like crazy, and I think we could be closer and have a whole lot hotter relationship if we got past this TV disagreement we are always having."

(Bill is listening, because his bride used the word "hotter.") Then state your needs without putting Bill on the defensive.

"Here's the thing, Bill. When you watch nineteen games per week and TiVo the others, I feel as if you don't care about me, even though I know you do."

Make a request, not a demand or an ultimatum, *à la*:

"If you don't turn that stupid game off I'm withholding sex, cooking, and laundry for a month. Go eat at your mother's!"

That might backfire just a little.

"Bill, can we hammer out a plan so you can watch lots of games, yet I can also get some of your undivided attention?"

(Bill, still all ears because you did say "lots of games.")

Talk about which games are most important to him. Maybe rank them in order of importance. If it's Game 7 of the Stanley Cup Finals, the guy is going to want to be fully engaged. I know with some people there is a hot game going on every night of the week. But there have to be limits.

Ask your man to consider choosing a time each day where the TV is always off and he is yours, all yours. Discuss the possibility of regular TV time for him, so he knows he can unwind and regroup while he watches. Talk about outings you could take, and be gracious enough to schedule these around important games and TV shows. (A romantic dinner may not unfold as you hoped during the Super Bowl.)

Tell him if he meets you halfway, the rewards will be rich. The closer you feel toward him, the nicer, sweeter, happier you will be. And you know what they say, a happy wife is a naked wife. Well, something like that.

The point is, when you tame the beast that TV can be, your relationship will blossom. And hey, while you're at it, don't let Suzy Kolber be the only woman your husband is interested in, just because she has a knack for deconstructing the play. If you can't beat 'em, plop down there on the sofa with 'em and ask for a one-on-one coaching session on the finer points of football (or hockey, baseball, basketball, soccer, etc.). You may never be the fan your guy is, but he will absolutely love it that you're trying.

Brenna: I find that our differences help balance each other out.

I can tell him to back off in certain situations and he tells me to come out of my shell a bit. We encourage each other.

Maggie: We are opposites!

He is quiet—I am a people person when I have to be! He is slow and I am fast. I can wing it—he gets flustered. I have to work on being patient and remember all the positives. Ugh! I have to pray for love and patience and kindness and remember that as annoyed as I am with him being slow and methodical and quiet and shy, he is just as annoyed about the way I am.

GIGO

So one of you is a party animal while the other loves to sit in solitude and watch grass grow. You're opposites— what a news flash! But how do an extrovert and an introvert mesh their different social styles, especially when the darling kiddies would prefer that no one ever did anything other than cater to their every whim? Read on.

Know Thyself . . . and Thy Man Too

Caroline and her husband have taken that first important step in melding their extrovert/introvert couplehood: simply getting more deeply what makes the other person tick. Caroline says:

My husband is very much an introvert whereas I am a social butterfly, which has brought about many interesting conversations and tense situations. When it comes to dealing with our different social styles I have just learned that he is a much happier man when he can have his own space, his surround sound, and/or his computer. From time to time he will have one of the guys over and he does see the benefit of socializing, but he doesn't thrive on it like I do.

I, on the other hand, love being around people and get very lonely, so we compromise by going out together on occasion or we just put it in the budget for me to go out with the girls every couple weeks so I don't go stir crazy.

Caroline gets that her husband needs alone time and lots of space, so that's what she tries to give him. She, on the other hand, will go bananas if she doesn't have regular outings with her girls. By the way, this couple lives in an apartment with their three little ones in a town near the Canadian arctic, where it's dark and wintry eight months out of the year. I admire that Caroline doesn't allow herself to get cooped up, even in those challenging circumstances. You go, girl!

Understand Your Spouse's Motivations

Step one is understanding whether your husband is a social animal or a shrinking Violet (Victor?). Most people are a mix of the two, but favor one or the other.

Next, dig deeper for your man's motivations. What makes his heart skip a beat? What makes your pulse pound?

Doyle and I, for example, have very different notions of our dream vacations. I would be overjoyed if suddenly Doyle wanted to go on a cruise or a guided tour of Europe, some getaway featuring an endless supply of new and interesting people to meet. When I bring this up he looks afraid. Trapped on a boat with a thousand people? No, Doyle would rather be breathing through a straw while being buried in sand by our five-year-old.

His fantasy vacation would be a big, manly hunting trip to the far north, with him hunting all day and me waiting for him in a cabin on the tundra, wearing a polar bear fur negligee. Can you see it? No, me neither. I'd be striking up conversations with trees in no time. And getting frostbite.

Big surprise then that our visions of a great time off on a Friday night are not all that similar. It wouldn't be fair for me to say to Doyle, "Hey, you've been busting your tokhes all week long at work. Let's go out with ten of our closest friends so you can unwind!"

Nor would it be equitable for him to suggest on a Friday night that he convene to the garage for five hours, tinkering with his bows and arrows in complete solitude. Often, a compromise is in order, which usually involves us stepping out as a couple for a movie or to Schuler's, our favorite bookstore/café, to browse in peace. We're still around people, which fulfills my social needs somewhat, yet Doyle can spend time "alone" watching the flick or with headphones strapped to his ears in the bookstore's music department.

Still, we have to be attuned to the fact that our guy may need more from time to time, a true scratching of the itch, so to speak. We tend to give people what we ourselves would like to receive. Love a night in, snuggled up in front of *Casablanca*? That may not be the ticket for your mate, who is jonesing for some cheering and hollering at the game. Instead, offer him an option that's in sync with how he sees the world.

When he feels truly chilled out and rested in his own singular way, he will also feel more connected to you. Real giving—extending yourself to give that which he truly, madly, deeply needs—is the gift that keeps on giving. He won't forget your sensitivity, and he'll feel genuinely loved and cared for. He'll know you get him, quirks and all. I'm not promising anything, but something tells me this act of selfless love may go both ways.

> When he feels truly chilled out and rested in his own singular way, he will also feel more connected to you.

Get Creative with Couple Time

Sometimes it just feels easier to ride with what your guy wants, doesn't it? Doing his thing all the time may strike you as submissive and self-sacrificing, traits befitting a nice church lady (albeit one with low-rise jeans). The truth is, neither one of you should let your needs slide time after time. Why? It's the easy way out, and it may even be passive aggressive. Sometimes, of course, selflessness is in order, but giving in too often eventually leads to resentment and bickering. Building your team of two is a better plan, so sit down and brainstorm activities you can do together.

One of the traps that many couples fall into is that as soon as one person makes a suggestion, the other person finds fault with it and then things deteriorate into an argument. So just throw out ideas, with a rule in place that no one is allowed to shoot down the other's plan for an outing (or "in-ing"). Enrich your couple time with activities that you can both get something out of.

Doyle would rather have his back waxed than attend a *Project Runway* season finale party. I would find a morning of sitting in the cold while waiting to shoot a deer to be mind-warpingly boring. So maybe Friday night I get my night off to watch a fashion design reality show with like-minded folk, humans with ovaries. And then Saturday morning he gets his thrills by sitting motionless in a tree stand for hours. But Saturday night may find the two of us together, watching a blues band perform at a music festival.

> Social Style A: Party Lady gets to say "Hey, girl" to a bunch of gal pals. Life is fun!
>
> Social Style B: Stoic Stud gets to say "Hey, buck" to a whitetail deer. Life is peaceful.
>
> Social Style A and Social Style B Mix It Up: Party and Stoic hold hands at a concert, their bond reinforced and their union on its way to becoming the smoldering volcano of torrid passion they always dreamed of. Hey, it could happen.

7

Money, Money, Money

Can come between me
and my honey, honey, honey

I'm not great with money.

There, I said it. Let's just lay that out on the table right away, lest anyone be deceived into thinking I am a grand financial adviser. But I know what it's like to fight with my husband about money, and how much that can eat away at our marriage. That's what really qualifies me to write this chapter, one I've been dreading (true confessions) since I first came up with the outline. Between you and me, writing this chapter on finances and marriage was a boon for my relationship with Doyle. As I gathered advice from real financial advisers and marriage experts, and learned so much from your stories about how cash flow affects your love match, a few things went *click* in my stubborn, thick head.

Money is not our number one bone of contention—that would be time off, see chapter 2—but when we do disagree about it, I find there's a surprising amount of pain and frustration involved. Why? Like many of you, I married my financial opposite. And many of you will say "Amen" to this statement: Our money "personalities" clash because of the under-the-skin financial baggage that existed even before we got married.

I will freely admit that I have more money baggage than Doyle. His parents, a cop and a stay-at-home mom who became a secretary when he was in high school, were never rolling in dough, but they essentially had enough to keep the bases covered. My mom stayed at home until I was fifteen, when she went back to work part time as a nurse. Looking back, I have no earthly idea of how we made ends meet before then, but a good guess would be that the Almighty helped us stretch the dollars we had and made it be enough.

My dad, you see, felt called to a ministry in the Christian bookstore business. He wanted to encourage his customers, and he had a passion for placing the right book or Bible in the right hands and for making a difference in people's lives through the printed word. It was a calling, a vocation, and he was the best in the world at it.

In following his calling, my dad gave my brother and me rich lives. We grew up between the shelves of his stores, the first one a downtown shop wedged between a massage parlor and a nightclub. Dan and I learned volumes about people, faith, evangelism, discipleship, and books, beautiful, wisdom-giving books.

We were affluent in a very real way, of this I have no doubt. As I write this, my dad died seven weeks ago, and our "wealthy" upbringing was underscored at his funeral, where hundreds lined up out the door of the church to pay tribute to the humble bookseller who touched so many lives. He followed his heart and loved his work, and in doing so, he was a booming success in many ways. My dad, Abe Reimer, was the king of booksellers, but he was never a businessman. The bookselling business is an uphill climb no matter what, but his ministry-first, business-later MO meant that neither store made much money.

We were pretty much strapped for cash from as far back as I can remember. But we always had enough food, a decent house, and a wood-paneled station wagon, the road trip machine that transported us to exotic locales such as Saskatchewan and South Dakota. Still, there were tensions and worries about how things would be paid for, especially big-ticket items such as braces and Christian school. The sacrifices my parents made for the bookstore and for us were endless, and I was always aware that they were made from a giving, loving heart.

But I've been afraid of struggling ever since. This has been at the base of tons of money clashes with me and Doyle. He wants to save and hoard and be prepared; I want to go to J. Jill and buy a new skirt, or to Old Navy and buy my daughter a pair of jeans, which she needs. (In his male mind, we females can get by wearing the skirts and jeans we have, never mind that one can't wear a summer skirt in October, or that Phoebe's 18-month jeans are now an inch too short.)

Essentially, that's how it goes around here. We have also fought about things such as Christian school for our kids. Doyle went to public school and hey, look how he turned out! That's his point. Mine is that we should be doing whatever we can to give our kids the very best education we can give them, just like my parents sacrificed to do for us.

Money, or the allocation of it, is at the root of this perennial disagreement. Why not tuck that huge chunk o' change in a retirement account, or even a college savings plan, my practical husband wonders. And hockey? My word, don't get me started. In my Manitoba childhood, ice rinks were as plentiful as snow in January and people sold equipment at garage sales. In the US, arenas are in short supply and hockey is an elite sport that costs an elite amount of cash. That's just the way it is. But hockey is in my blood, and I love it. Jonah loves it too, and so I think the obscene amount of money is worth it.

Okay, so I got started. Anyway, suffice it to say Doyle doesn't think the obscene amount of money is worth it, and we've had words to that effect.

Here's the deal: Fighting about money is as old as money itself, arising partly out of philosophical differences and partly from habits so old you forgot you had them. When you have your first baby, you're in sticker shock at all the ways that bundle of joy can wreak havoc on your wallet. The costs of a new baby can reach from

$9,000 to $11,000! There's the nursery, the car seat, the furniture . . . the list goes on, even if you're frugal.

Experts say that having kids also leads to a time crunch that sets you up for more spending on restaurant meals, household help, and many purchases, since you have less leisure to comparison shop. (This is true for me. I have a hard time contrasting the price of cereals when one kid is trying to climb out of the shopping cart and the other one is begging for the priciest, most sugar-laden breakfast foods known to mankind.)

> Experts say that having kids also leads to a time crunch that sets you up for more spending.

There are many aspects of life with kids that have hefty price tags. Stay at home versus day care; maternity leave versus staying home; start the college fund now or later. The choices—and arguments—are endless.

With each child added to the family, the financial pie gets sliced again, often leaving slivers to quibble over. Debt, allocation of funds, investing, and other cash-related topics are often the biggest source of marital antagonism, with or without kids.

"Ron would nickel-and-dime me about my spending if he thought he could get away with it," says Angie, mom of four. "The other night he got mad at me because of a report he saw on TV about finding inexpensive instruments for your kids. He said I should have better researched the process of buying a flute for Anna, even though I got a good deal—a year ago. It's things like this that cause us to fight over money and how we spend it on our kids. Kids are expensive—especially four of them!"

When those pie slices get smaller and smaller, many couples find themselves duking it out over their financial choices in a way they never did before.

Thanks to the new expenses they found themselves saddled with during the first few months following their daughter Tallie's birth, Scott and his wife, Louanne, fell into a regular pattern of arguing about money. "If I'd buy myself a pair of golf shoes, she'd complain that she couldn't buy herself a new purse," Scott says. "We'd always end up tense and upset. It came down to who was choosing to do what with the little bit we had left over."

Adding fuel to the fire is that, when it comes to money issues, you often come at the issue from completely different directions. A spender like your husband will pick a saver like you. This kind of pairing can actually be beneficial because you can neutralize each other. If the two of you were spendthrifts, you would never save anything. If you were both hoarders you would never take risks or get a better house or do anything fun. Can a happy compromise be worked out?

You know we'll go over all that in GIGO, but for now, let's sort out some of the hottest of the hot money topics for moms and dads. Of all the answers given by the moms who responded to my survey, four heated issues rose to the top as the most contentious cash conundrums:

Stacey: He spoils our kids.

Just last night, our four-year-old son, Alex, broke his light saber. He says to me, "Mom, look it's broke. I guess I'll have to tell Dad to get me another one!"

Julie: My in-laws made my husband work too hard for everything and now he talks all the time about what our kids will have to work for.

Probably our biggest money argument is that I don't want to make a long list of "what we're not going to pay for" for the kids. My husband likes to make random comments such as, "We are definitely not going to pay for their cars." Since our kids are currently only three and one, we do not need to cross that bridge just yet! Maybe someday we'll help them by paying for some part of a car, or loan them some of the money because I want to know that the boys are driving something safe and not a total beater that won't get them safely somewhere. Why does my husband go on about this stuff when it's so far into the future? I feel that my in-laws made him work too hard for everything and didn't help him enough. They almost promoted the notion of "you can buy anything you want if you are paying for it." So now he has it fixed in his mind that he's going to do the same thing with our kids. I totally disagree!

Lisa: My husband spends too much on frivolous things.

The biggest point of contention is his ability to spend money on golf pretty comfortably and regularly, while I (the keeper of the purse strings!) have to remind him that $500 for a "men only" golf trip to Baltimore takes a big chunk out of our family budget!

Becky: My husband wants me to work but I want to stay home.

Our biggest issue probably. I want to stay home ... forever. He thinks I should get a job (full time) as soon as the kids are in school full time. Ugh! It kills me to think I won't be able to be involved in school activities, etc. My hubby works a lot, usually fifty hours a week, plus two hours drive time round trip. I think one of us needs to be available full time for the kids. He doesn't want to continue to make the sacrifices that come with being a one-income family. And it does get harder every year. The economy doesn't support one-income families.

Dish Panel

Beyond the four biggest issues, my dish girls were all over the map about the currency matters that make them and their guy crabby at each other.

Angela: I feel like we're practically living hand to mouth.

My husband and I fight about money constantly. He won't stick to a budget and we barely save anything, even though we both have pretty good jobs. And now he wants to buy a bigger house because interest rates are low. I'm terrified of taking out a huge mortgage but he says I'm being irrational. Maybe so, but what about saving for the kids' college and our retirement? I feel like we'll practically be living hand to mouth. This issue is ruining our relationship.

Caroline: Jason wasn't convinced at first that cloth diapers would be worth it.

One of the bigger money arguments we have had was over switching to cloth diapers from disposables. Jason wasn't convinced (at first) that the extra hassle and the initial investment was worth it, but in the long run we both were shocked at how much we saved on garbage bags, wipes (we now use baby washcloths), Diaper Genie refills, and then the cost of diapers for three children.

Tenny: We both like expensive toys.

My husband's the power tools kind of guy while I'm the scrapbooking girl. Both are hobbies that can eat up some serious dough. We try to find out what is needed (i.e., a certain tool so that we can fix our roof) and what is not needed but desired (i.e., the newest scrapbooking die-cut machine), and then we weigh the two. We usually know the answer: *save money*. I think the biggest thing is that we should agree to save. If that means do-it-yourself projects on the house so that it's livable, and no "toys" (or no anniversary presents), that's fine. Our end goal is the same even if we both have doubts about how to get there along the way.

K: We no longer argue about money.

We are of a mind-set that money is ours to control, not to let it control us, and since we have made that change we no longer argue about money. We are a one-income family, so we have to agree with how any extra is being spent, and constant discussion and checks and balances allow us to be sure we are on the same page.

Melinda: Sometimes I wish I had more to spend on myself.

I feel like I can't spend on myself since the two little darlings came around. Granted, I'd rather do without so that they are pampered silly. But it has been years since I visited a front-door store to buy something for myself. At times, I'm a little bitter in a very sixty-second selfish sort of way, because I remember when money wasn't an issue way back in the day. It would just be nice to shop in a store that didn't have price scanners throughout and a six-item-or-less line, and where my underwear didn't get sticky on the conveyor belt.

Lisa: I wish my husband would take over our finances.

The only disagreement we have about money is who should actually be the financial person in the marriage. I think Dan should, as the head of our household, but he really has no interest or ability. He's a physical therapist, so he has a clinician mind-set. Business and money are *so* not his thing! When I was working full time, I was in a corporate environment. So I get it by default.

GIGO

As my dish ladies have so eloquently articulated, there are all kinds of thorny issues when it comes to cash. I think it's pretty rare that two people come to a marriage with identical or even close financial viewpoints, which can lead to big friction. Here's hoping that the tips in GIGO will help you figure out how to have the best of both money styles. It "just" takes some finesse, patience, and understanding.

It's Not All about the Benjamins

Tiffs over money are often really about other stuff. "Money can be a vehicle for conflict and hurt. For example, a person who is angry about sex might withhold money," says therapist and divorce mediator Lois Gold. "It's not what the conflict is about that causes a break-up, it's how the conflict was handled. Each person needs to be heard and understood."[1]

Hire a babysitter and spend an evening discussing your feelings about money. (Call it a "budget meeting" if you think that will raise less in the way of red flags.) Hash through what makes you afraid when it comes to money, and what you hope your family's income can accomplish. For example, you might be worried that you don't have enough of a cushion in case of catastrophe, or fretful that in your golden years the two of you will be sharing a can of cat food and sucking on bouillon cubes whilst living under a bridge somewhere.

On the dream end, you may harbor fond wishes for a new bathtub, a trip to Australia, or a fine college education for the youngsters.

When you figure out what emotions lie beneath your money issues, you'll better grasp what you truly value.

You may find out that your husband's core issue is feeling like he is providing a safety net for your family for whatever may come. Your personality may be the opposite, as in, "Let tomorrow take care of itself. Let's have fun today." But if you never have these important little confabs, you'll never realize these key differences. When you grasp your guy better, and he comprehends you, it will help you become much stronger partners in the money department.

Don't Leave the Other Person in the Dark

Guilty. Yes, I am very, very guilty of this. It's tempting to just do everything my own way because it seems so much easier. I've got my system in place and I don't want anyone, even my beloved, tinkering with it. But even if one partner—in our case, me—usually handles the money maintenance (i.e., paying the bills, dealing with the bank), it can leave the other guy/girl in the dark without a clear picture of the family's financial situation.

The more open I am about our expenses and our loose change, the happier my man is. Who doesn't hate to be kept out of the loop, especially about such an important issue? Having regular cash chitchats will be a boon for your love life, I can tell you from experience! Some money talking points:

Talk about how your parents viewed money. This can offer a lot of insight into your own and your guy's spending views.

Discuss your goals and values when it comes to saving and spending, and try to find common ground (see below).

Monthly or even weekly, take turns balancing the checkbook, or simply spend five minutes every month going over it together.

Hammer Out a Plan

Ugh. I hate financial planning! I'd rather be nominated for *What Not to Wear* than to grit (gnash?) my teeth and pore over money details. But it's one of those unpleasant—to me, anyway—investments that must be made in order for a big payoff: closing the canyon between two financial opposites and your contrasting hopes and dreams for your money.

He feels a new garage roof would be the best use of your money, and you think he's crazy. Who cares about the garage roof when you are yearning for mosaic tiles on your bathroom floor? One night of discussing where you would both like to see your money spent, and coming to some kind of compromise you can both live with, will pay out big dividends for your financial picture *and* your relationship. Just ask Stephanie:

> I've wanted a new kitchen for eight years, but I know it will be at least another two to three years before it gets done. We've decided together that remodeling the bathrooms will take priority over fixing up the kitchen. I'm okay with this because I've had a say in making the plan for what household things get done and when. So I'm not getting a new kitchen, but I am getting two new

bathrooms that I don't have to scrub nasty, moldy grout in anymore. It takes a lot of time to make a plan, but the time spent is worth it because it gives us a sense of accomplishment (we built a plan) and it takes pressure off my husband who insists on doing all the work himself, and it helps me know I really won't have to wait forever for the kitchen. The plan is not written in stone and can be changed as needed, but we both need to agree to it.

Think Up a New Name for the "B" Word, and Then Do It

Oooh, I hate the word *budget*. It makes my skin crawl. It makes me itch. It makes me feel like I've developed a rash. Most of all, budget talk makes me feel controlled, reined in, suffocated. See, I'm very loosey-goosey in this way. I am a free spirit when it comes to money. Some months I wouldn't mind keeping a lid on the spending, and other months I mind very much. To suggest that I need to stick to a set amount each month just backfires, especially when that suggestion comes packaged in the word *budget*. Weird, I know. But there you are. Thus, I've been trying to turn that word and concept inside out and make it work for loosey-goosey, free-spirited *moi*.

It's a bit of a stretch, but I can, in the interest of financial peace and a warm, potentially canoodling relationship with Mr. Can't-We-Please-Make-a-Budget? work out a ballpark, sketchy figure of how much I need each month. This figure won't be exhaustive or in-depth, because there is nothing about me that is detailed. I can have freedom within that number, yet Black-and-White Man finds solace in knowing it's a predictable figure.

Seven Ways to Have Those Special Little Chats

Talking about money is hard, much harder than fighting. So if it takes a while to replace debates with discussions, don't sweat it. Even if you do it wrong, it's better to communicate than to not say anything. Make it your new motto: Stop fightin', keep talkin'. (Make love, not war . . .)

1. **Take a hike.** Or a walk. Men don't like to open up about this, so having the discussion while you're relaxed, out in the fresh air, will help.
2. **"In the Kublachefski clan, we always buried our savings under the old oak tree . . ."** What were your family's attitudes toward money? What were the financial dynamics at your house? Tell your guy about you first, and then ask him about his own kin. This will be illuminating, I promise you.
3. **Humility goes a long way.** Don't shoot the guy down as soon as he mentions his desire to take out a second mortgage, quit his job, and open a bait shop annexed to your house. Ask him to also keep an open mind. Keep it light, as always. "Stanley, my studmuffin, let's play a little game here where the first person to interrupt the other person has to drop and do ten push-ups." Well, you get the drift, right? Just don't assume it's your way or no way, because you may as well pack it in right there and then if you don't have some humility. Listen to what the man says and take it in. His outlook may differ wildly from yours, but he holds his views as dearly as you hold yours, so be respectful, even if you disagree.
4. **"Someday we'll have to send Homer to Harvard."** Experts say the worst fights couples have boil down to the fact that they haven't planned their big-picture goals yet. This makes everyone involved feel uneasy and stressed out. Discuss various milestones in your life that will require money—having more kids, buying a house, college, caring for a parent, etc.

5. **Bond over the bank deposit box.** Sounds crazy, but you guys will become oh-so-attached to one another when you have a project you can both get excited about, such as saving for an anniversary weekend at a bed-and-breakfast, or a houseboat vacation for next summer. Every payday, lop off a set amount and deposit it into a special account. The feeling of success will be a new financial bond between you!

6. **Make it an outing.** Go to a financial seminar together, like Dave Ramsey's Financial Peace seminars. It'll be an outing for just the two of you, and you'll get lots of food for thought to mull over together at dinner that night.

7. **Don't lay blame, take action.** Let's say your partner is in debt. Rather than fight about it (Hello: Arguing won't reduce that monthly payment!), force yourselves to focus on a game plan. Blaming puts space and distance and resentment between you, while taking steps to address the problem will remind you that you are, and always will be, a financial team.

Split the Leftovers for "Mad Money"

After you've gotten real with each other and figured out how much is going toward fixed expenses (mortgage, utilities, chocolate . . .), split any leftover money, with each of you having the right to spend his or her share in any way. You'll find that his fishing lures and your mani-pedi go a long way to bringing you guys to your respective happy place.

Hopefully, after reading through other moms' experiences, you learned a thing or two about working together on this major element of any marriage. I think I can honestly say my research has helped me out. Doyle and I just went shopping for a minivan about an hour ago, and we kind of had a good time! (Although I did have to point out the clear difference between teal and forest green, and how teal is desirable while forest green is totally 1991.) My point is, we have gotten a better grasp on how to talk about money and not get so tense. Now if I could only persuade him to go for that teal minivan we'd be in business.

8

When Your Ovaries Twitch at the Sight of Footie PJs

Working it out when you want more kids and he doesn't

"I can't stand looking at baby clothes," I recently told Doyle as we were being sofa spuds together, watching the telly.

"Why?" he said, puzzled.

"Because I just love little babies, and there is just this pull to have another one that I can't even explain. I know it doesn't make any sense."

His eyes widened, and thankfully our show returned from commercial break. I knew he didn't get it and probably never would. I had been putting off having an endometrial ablation for months, even though most of the time I felt "done" having kids. "With three kids we have reached maximum capacity," I would tell people if they asked whether we were "done." (There's that word again.)

We have three beautiful, strong-willed, active children who keep us running from morning until night. Another baby would be insane, yet I do have moments when I crave the feeling of holding a teeny, tiny, floppy-necked baby, snuggly in footie pjs and fresh from God himself.

A recent spate of friends having their last babies has not helped matters, I must say. Yet I know, on the whole, that our family is complete. Doyle's been meaning to go visit Dr. Snippy and make the whole thing a moot point. I wish he would so I could finally put this bizarre desire for another baby to rest.

Lisa can relate to my capricious feelings: "As of late, I've really felt the ridiculous pull of wanting just one more baby," she said. "However, my age (39) and my husband's vasectomy have, for all intents and purposes, ended that discussion! (When I bring up the 'what ifs' of having another baby, Dan always jokingly tells me, 'This store is closed!' or 'Ma'am, that line has been discontinued!') So we're going to get a puppy next spring instead!"

Since we already have Dinah, a high-maintenance basset hound, perhaps a kitten would scratch the itch of baby cravings. I'll keep you posted on that, but basically our "store" is closed too, and our line is discontinued.

Sometimes the issue of more kids or not is harder to solve, especially when one of you wants another little person around and the other one doesn't. I've heard of the guy wanting more kids and his wife being the one to put the brakes on the procreation train, but generally speaking it's often the woman who gets those one-more-baby blues. (If your situation is the former, that your hub wants more kids and you're done, you can still apply the lessons learned from these stories and tips. Forgive me for my generalizing, but statistics bear me out: Most of the time Mom wants more and Dad doesn't.)

Take Stephen and Clare. They already had two boys, ages seven and eight, and for a long time they thought their baby days were over. When Clare started having fantasies about having a baby girl, it didn't make sense to Stephen at all. "We'd survived the diaper years, the sleepless nights, the baby in the bed beside us, and finally, with our sons sleeping in their own rooms through the night, I had the love of my life back to myself," he said.

Oops, Clare got pregnant after a night of vacation nookie, and she was thrilled. Stephen? Not so much. He balked at the idea of lugging baby stuff everywhere, no sex for weeks and weeks, and especially the huge life changes and sacrifices the baby would bring. For one, he would cut back on hours devoted to his business and become a stay-at-home dad again. He felt they couldn't afford another baby, he was too old to start over again, and hey, they were incredibly happy the way they were.

But there she was, the incontrovertible fact of Lily, growing in her mother's womb and tearing her mommy and daddy apart. They fought. She cried. "Our relationship had become a living hell," Stephen said. Clare was over the moon when she found out for sure she would be getting her girl. But Stephen's lack of interest in the baby made her feel increasingly lonely, and her lack of understanding of his feelings made him depressed.

When it came time for Lily's birth, Clare had asked Stephen not to be with her—that's how miles apart this once-close couple was. "It's hard to admit to friends you are having a child your husband doesn't want," Clare said.

After some painful hours of labor and the prospect of a C-section, Clare finally caved in and let the nurses call Stephen to come be with her. He walked into the delivery room still stubbornly opposed to letting a baby hijack his life again. Then Lily was there, not just a theoretical hassle but pink, and gorgeous, and his. "I held her in my arms, and for the third time in my life, my heart left my body."[1]

You may be tempted to cue up lullaby music and picture this little family sailing off into the sunset happily ever after. What really happened was this: Even though Stephen fell in love with his baby, and he realized what a blessing she was, the two still grappled with his resistance to another child. Clare had to come to terms with the fact that her husband needed to be honest about how he felt, and he in turn had to face the realities he was dreading. In some ways, their family took a step backward financially, time-wise, and in their long-term goals. The baby was still a lot of work, she kept them up at night, their sex life probably took a nosedive, and she still required big sacrifices on all their parts. Things didn't magically adjust without much effort from Stephen and Clare.

Why do I recount their saga for you? Because it's such a real and honest story of how Mom and Dad can be pitted against one another when one (let's face it, usually Mom) wants another baby and the other partner doesn't. I take this issue especially seriously, because one of my oldest friends in the world divorced her husband because he wouldn't relent to her pleas to have more than one child. Listen to my friend's words just shortly before her marriage ended:

> I don't think Ron has ever really adjusted to fatherhood, and Amara is six! As a matter of fact, he said only a few months ago that he is only now starting to enjoy Amara and that he hated her babyhood. I found this comment offensive and hurtful, and it seems to be his way of saying once again that he doesn't want another baby. That's all I want, is another baby! We've both changed so much and we've gone in very different directions, and yes, these changes occurred within the first couple of months after Amara was born. We haven't been the same to each other since becoming parents.

Oh, that's just so sad. There was more to it than that, of course, but my dear friend believes her husband's unwillingness to have another child was the core issue behind their divorce. It's just a huge matter, enormous, because it means one partner is hitting a brick wall when it comes to the core of her heart's desires.

Why do some guys just not want to add another precious bundle to their clan? For tons of reasons, including these three rationales:

Angie: My husband was an only child and never wanted more than one.

Although he knew I wanted three, he wanted one, agreeing to a second even though he felt very anxious about it. He does not understand what it's like to have a sibling. I have two siblings and I think three is the best number of kids to have.

Britney: My husband is worried about not being able to provide adequately for a third child.

When Dave and I got married we both wanted three or four. But now he has changed his mind. He wants two. I still want three. He is nervous about not being able to provide a third with a college education, for example.

Carla: My husband thinks another baby would cut too much into his hobbies.

We already have a hard time juggling his need to be out in the woods shooting something or fishing for something with my need to paste die-cuts into a scrapbook. The two kids we have are getting to a more manageable age where they are not so high maintenance. I very much want one more, but he is putting his foot down.

Lots of guys wrestle with the emotional, spiritual, and financial responsibility of increasing their families. They worry too, like Carla's hub, that one more child will take time away from their pursuits. And like Steven, they fret that a baby will take the woman they love away from them even more than she already is.

The thing is, they are completely, totally, absolutely right.

Babies and kids are total time pits (you know, like remodeling a Victorian farmhouse is a money pit). And come to think of it, the little cherubs are money pits too. Somehow men are able to be much more rational and practical about these things. We mamas not so much. When our ovaries start to twitch within a hundred yards of a baby sleeping in his mother's arms, for example, all objectivity flies out the window.

Another factor: when those old eggs ain't quite as fresh as they used to be, speaking of ovaries, we see that window of opportunity closing, and we suddenly have all these crazy thoughts about doing it all over again. The rooster in the home (running with the poultry analogy), on the other hand, has no such abdomen-clutching, heart-jumping, sentimental seizures. His internal organs don't lurch at the sight of terry cloth footie pajamas with darling bunnies on the toes. I'm just saying.

Dish Panel

So, the issue is complicated, weighty, and sometimes heart wrenching. And many factors influence how each partner feels. Snoop at the door of my dish panel here and find out how some of these ladies came to their decisions about the size of their families.

Julie: Our first child almost didn't make it, so I feel blessed to have the two I have.

Our first child had a traumatic birth. So after enduring a nonmedicated C-section to get him out and all of his tests to rule out scary problems, I just felt blessed to have him. I almost didn't dare ask God for another healthy baby after that. During my second pregnancy I kept praying for a normal, healthy placenta and baby. After a preplanned C-section (with a spinal epidural!), I had a healthy little guy. I am very content with two. If someone were to drop off a little girl on our doorstep, though, I would love her to pieces!

Did she say nonmedicated C-section? I am shuddering!

Stephanie: Everyone was here who was meant to be here, including our lost baby.

When my son was two I had a late-term miscarriage at nineteen weeks. It took another year to get pregnant, this time with our daughter. When we started to talk about if we wanted more children, something about another one didn't seem to fit. It seemed to me everyone was here who was meant to be here and a part of our family, including our lost baby.

K: I had something/someone telling me to just open my mind to thinking about having one more child.

After I had my second child by C-section, I no longer wanted any more. We had both a boy and a girl and felt we should be happy and blessed with what we had been given. My hubby wanted more; he really wanted to try one more time but respected that I had to go through a lot to have them, so in the end it would be my decision. I can only say that I had a "God" experience about two years ago, and I felt something/someone telling me to just open my mind to thinking about having one more child. I did, and once my praying and seeking led me to believe it was the right choice, I told hubby, and he was beyond excited. We decided to leave it up to God and try for one more, but we would only try till my birthday. If nothing, then my hubby would get snipped. I was pregnant in a month! God is good.

Katrina: My husband finally decided to try for a fourth baby, but his timing couldn't have been worse!

After our third child, I immediately wanted to have a fourth (I mentioned it in the delivery room), but my hub was not into it at all. I didn't pester him, but we did talk about it at different times and Chris was reticent—possibly overwhelmed at the prospect. The summer after Kipp was born, we went camping with my husband's family. We were there setting up, waiting for his parents to pull in with their rig. My husband came over and gave me a little squeeze as his parents backed into their spot and said, "I really think I'm ready to try for another." I looked at him with the deepest love in my eyes and said, "You are such a dork! Why would you rob yourself of a great opportunity by telling me this at a campground surrounded by your family and a million strangers?" Later on I did reward his courage, but we have yet to be blessed by another child. We are trusting God on this and just enjoying the three we have, believing that these good gifts are what he has for us.

After seven years with three boys, Katrina and her husband recently caught the adoption bug and are planning a trip to Zambia in a few months to adopt a baby girl!

GIGO

Back Off

If you want another baby with every fiber of your being, you may be tempted to be one pushy broad to persuade your husband to make the family's quiver fuller. But pushing and shoving—verbally, at least—is going to backfire in a big way. Instead, realize the hugeness of this for your husband—he's going to have to invest masses of his own backbreaking, heartbreaking parenting energy into this potential baby. He may be scared, confused, and tense. Ramming your agenda through on an issue as delicate and complex as this will probably be a deal breaker. Instead, give ground to your sweetie so he can think and pray through this decision, like Diana did:

I dreamed of a third child, but Eric felt adamantly that two was good. I tried not to push it—which is a challenge for me! I just tried to talk to him about it when I felt it was a good time. We had some of the most serious conversations we have ever had. Finally, he asked that I leave him alone completely and let him think about whether we should have a third or not. He said that's what he really, really needed: time. I thought that was reasonable so I walked away from this and gave him as much time as he needed. In the end he decided that yes, another child would benefit our family. I guess I got "my way," but I don't think he would have responded well if I had badgered him about it. It probably would have damaged our relationship.

Your guy may not respond as favorably as Eric did, but it's key to give him the time and space he needs to hash through it all.

Listen Like You Mean It

A big part of loving someone well is sharing the deepest parts of our hearts, and then setting that aside as much as possible to hear the heart of the one we adore. Tell your guy you want to really *get* the fears and worries he has about increasing your family. Let him talk for a good chunk of time without jumping in every five minutes. (Oh, was I just talking to myself again? Oops.) Do ask him questions that help you both clarify his trepidation. The goal here is understanding the guy you love in a deeper way, not necessarily agreeing on having a baby or not having one.

Find a Mentor Couple

Talk to a couple who has also tussled with whether or not to have more kids, and see what they found helpful in making their decision. How to broach such a private matter? First, ask around in your inner circle of family and friends. Did anyone go through this impasse in their own marriage? Chances are excellent someone did, or one of your trusted pals or your sister-in-law knows someone who did. You could also ask your minister or another older and wiser source to give you a lead.

Know That It's Not Just Black and White

Do you feel as if the only two choices are both bad ones? Either you give in and give up your dream of another child, or your husband caves and gives you what you want? I guess a third option would be to continue on the impasse you're in. A stalemate is kind of like concrete: it hurts when you keep knocking your head against it! All of the above are great ways to weaken your bond. Don't look at this as an either-or scenario: "Either he 'lets' me have this baby or I'm going to be sad and mad for a loooong time." You're just setting yourself up for disappointment and resentment, or you're positioning your man for the same thing.

What this really is, believe it or not, is a chance to brace and bolster your union through this difficult passage and beyond. Marriage counselors Gary and Carrie Oliver concur that the issue at stake here is not really baby or no baby, even though it feels that way. "It's about what it looks like to serve, cherish, and encourage each other in the context of dealing with an emotionally charged issue," they say. "This 'problem' is a great opportunity for you to improve your communication, cultivate new listening skills, better understand when your emotions can and can't be trusted, deepen your trust and intimacy, and increase your oneness with God. Then you'll be able to make a mutually satisfying decision."[2]

Whatever happens, even if you decide to go with his desire to quit procreating (or adopting), it's not the end of the world. Honestly. Maybe, like I did quite recently, you'll wake up one day and realize you really are done, and that's okay. Perhaps it will be the day your two-year-old decides that toasting paper in the toaster oven is a good idea. That's my story! Or it could be that you just come to a place of deciding to focus on the family and marriage you already have. You may always regard babies a bit wistfully, but someday you'll realize that's just you—a baby aficionado—and it doesn't mean you have to raise another one. And one more thought: Watch and see how God fills up the empty spaces. He wants you and your husband to love each other well more than he wants you to have another baby. He will always fill you up in just the way you need.

9

Get It Goin' On Again, Sister Friend

The fun, naked part of revving up your marriage

So, you've negotiated your differences in discipline.

The rope has gone slack on your time-off tug-o-war.

Your Mama Bear has dulled her roar, and you've given your man more leeway in his parenting. You've . . .

reached a deal that works for both of you in terms of division of labor;

cooperated with each other in your opposite social styles and needs;

settled on the money matters that used to make you unsettled;

navigated together the sticky wickets of in-laws and out-laws;

traversed the big hurdle of one of you wanting a baby and the other one wanting to run screaming in the other direction . . .

Now there is only one thing to do: Disrobe. Unleash. Partake of some lovin', touchin', and squeezin'. (Thank you, Journey, for that great song title!)

Yes, we're big girls and I won't mince words. Nookie is what you need, my friend, lots of good old-fashioned nookie. I know you have eighteen objections jumping up and down, hands raised, clamoring for your attention. If they could talk—and you won't let them, will you?— they'd mention fatigue, exhaustion, lack of sex drive, kiddies bursting in at inopportune moments. They'd be on the money about most of it. But—stick with me here, girls—you can turn your back on those pesky little naysayer voices in your head that tell you why the passionate life is not for you.

It is for you. You are a red-hot mama whether or not you know it yet. And once you let that hot side of you free, she'll revitalize you in ways you never dreamed of. Because the truth of the matter is, great sex energizes rather than depletes you. It conveys love and affection, soothes, comforts and relaxes, and relieves stress outside and inside of your relationship.

Passion bridges the gap when inevitable relationship conflicts flare, and it enhances closeness. Most of all, when that red hot mama inside of you is activated, you are reminded that you're more than a meat-cutting, squabble-settling, sock-matching robot. You become playful, flirty, and sensual, the way God created you to be.

Regular action between the sheets is also a great way to realize that you and your husband are not roommates or platonic friends who happen to share the same children.

I always tell the story of one mom who told me she felt as if her husband was becoming like a brother to her. She loved him, but she also loved her brothers. *Oh my*. Scary, but actually not unheard of in our oddly asexual personas as moms. It's so incredibly easy to slide into complacency when it comes to revving up our sexual engines.

Passion bridges the gap when inevitable relationship conflicts flare, and it enhances closeness.

And after complacency, that sputtering engine grinds to a halt in a sad place called "no sparks." Planet Platonic. Roommates-ville.

What I told this dear young mother was to hop in the shower as soon as humanly possible—with her extremely naked, not-her-brother, used-to-make-her-stomach-flip man. Nudity, I believe, is a great antidote to feeling brotherly love toward the lawfully wedded man in your life. A picture is worth a thousand words, and hopefully the sight of her husband in his birthday suit said, "We are not related" in a thousand different ways.

Of course, getting sudsy in the shower is just a stop-gap measure. There needs to be little spark-plug, flip-switcher maneuvers happening regularly to get the old mojo going again. If you're as busy as I think you are, chances are that work, kids, and both your jam-packed schedules are putting the squeeze on the oh-so-sweet private time you two share, and throwing a wet blanket on that fiery goddess of love lurking within you.

That's why you have to start flipping the switch with little get-connected gestures over and over again. Even if sex and passion and romance are now the last things on your checklist, when you add a few quickie bonding rituals to your daily routine, you'll be amazed at how interested you'll become.

Okay, so maybe you don't feel like yanking your five-year-old negligee out of the back of your drawer. You don't have any desire to resume your previously smoldering-volcano-of-torrid-lust pre-kid days. As one mom told me, forget blazing volcanoes, her love life resembled "a flickering molehill." So fake it. Pretend you are interested, and see what happens.

One bored mama I knew stuck a lacy thong in her husband's briefcase just for the heck of it. She had seen some sex therapist on a talk show who suggested this as a way of reclaiming passion. All day long she wondered what her husband's reaction had been to the thong. Had he been pleased?

Is Canada cold? Yes, of course the man was overjoyed. But the interesting thing was what happened to the wife as she became more and more tickled about her little surprise. She didn't start out the day "in the mood" for anything. Basically, she threw the thing in there on a whim. But by the time her man got home from work the pump was primed, if you get my meaning. And her husband acted as if he had won the Powerball. She could have served burned mac n' cheese and cold hot dogs for dinner and the guy wouldn't have cared.

Flip That Switch

Getting going is half the battle, so take a cue from Mrs. Thong. Sometimes it's up to us to flip those switches and get those lights turned on again. Even if we don't feel particularly romantic, we can regrow that part of ourselves. Remember, romance is about details and small, meaningful gestures. Try a few of these easy, flirty moves and see if you're not getting warmer and warmer with each one!

1. Write "I love you" on his plate in ketchup or some other squeezable condiment. (Cheesy? Yes. You're catching on, sister friend. Squeezable cheese works too!)
2. Put heart-shaped ice cubes in his drinks.
3. Iron a Superman decal onto his boxers—just because.
4. Rent the first movie you ever saw together. (Ours was *Days of Thunder* with Tom Cruise and Nicole Kidman. Yeah, depressing!)
5. Make him a CD of romantic songs you both love.
6. While grocery shopping, grab one completely impractical, pricey snack item that he loves.
7. Put a candy heart in his jacket pocket once a week.
8. Draw a cute picture of the two of you with crayons and tape it to the fridge.
9. Wear a picture of him in a locket around your neck.
10. "Write" sweet messages on his back with your fingers.

11. Enter sweet messages into his Palm Pilot's calendar (e.g., 2:00 p.m.—"I Want U"; 3:00 p.m.—"UR Hot").
12. Laugh at his jokes, even if they're not really funny.
13. Pat his butt when he passes you in the hall.

Every union has stored-up emotional energy. And although these flip-switchers are pretty easy, they all add fuel to that relationship tank. When you draw a heart on the bathroom mirror or laugh at his corny joke, you're storing it up. Then when your marriage is under stress, you'll have the oomph you need to get through.

Guys Take It Sooooo Personally When We Say No

A vital little notation here: Guys view sex far differently than we do. And how. We already know they are Martians and we are Venusians. We get, hopefully, that our men will never have the same ideas about timing as we do. ("Uh, your parents are coming over in ten minutes and the dog just barfed . . . this is actually *not* a good time for wild, passionate sex!") There are effective ways to deal with times when his timing is off, and faking a headache isn't one of them.

But I would be remiss if I didn't take this chance to underscore the fact that guys often take our rejections in the sack quite personally. Even if we are bone tired, sick of being touched, grabbed, and mauled all day long by our kids, and desperate for some alone time with a juicy novel, our guys can take a rejection as meaning "I don't want you in any way, shape, or form.

I wouldn't want you if you were the last man on a deserted island (although the deserted island sounds good about now)."

Listen to one guy's real-life lament: "I've accepted that I want to have sex more than she does, but I won't apologize for being attracted to my wife and having sexual needs. I feel let down and unwanted every time she turns me down."

Unless your hub's self esteem is extremely high, he may personalize your rebuffs, even if you have a valid reason for skipping hanky panky on a given night. He may not be able to accept a no at face value. This means we have to be savvy when it comes to turning our guy down. We have to be honest about what's going on in our lives, yet clearly demonstrate that they are still tempting, pleasing, alluring, and wanted. We have to give them hope. The order of the day, then, is the facts, lined with silvery optimism and delivered with cushy warmth.

"Charlie, *muffin* (insert cutesy food nickname of your choice), could you be a prince and take a rain check? You know, today was kind of grueling with the triplets knocking over the lobster tank at the grocery store. I feel like I have a touch of post-traumatic stress syndrome. But hey, tomorrow night let's try this idea I was reading about in a magazine, you know the one!"

Or . . .

"Freddie, *bagel*, love of my life, listen. Since I went to bed so late watching the Tigers game with you last night, and the baby got up so early, I am barely keeping my eyes open. I don't think I'd be very much fun tonight at all. If I get my beauty sleep, though, I think tomorrow night I will get my energy back—and then some!"

Or . . .

"Howie, *croissant*, for some strange, incomprehensible reason, I don't think I am up for a night of raging ardor, even though I find you as hunky as ever. My doctor says my 'take me now' hormones will kind of flatten out from time to time, depending on my cycle. But just give me a couple of days here and I think the mood will return— with interest!"

You get my point. Even if you never, ever refer to your husband as a carbohydrate product, you can still give him a spoonful of sugar when you are asking him to swallow that pill of rejection (i.e., no futon fandango for him). This method of dealing with unwanted advances actually brings you nearer and dearer as opposed to pulling you apart like the old-school way. This also prevents the vicious cycle we all know so well:

You're not in the mood,

so you reject him in some cold or passive way (i.e., sneaking upstairs early for bed),

hence making him feel unloved,

thus hurting him unnecessarily,

therefore driving a wedge between you,

consequently causing him to possibly act unloving toward you,

and as a result, you are *less* in the mood than you were when you first kicked him to the curb!

Yes, when you use this tried and true method of come-on management, things will turn out differently. Let's say you're tired/stressed/just plain not into it. You lovingly tell him what's going on, being careful to safeguard his feelings and outline a plan for future lovemaking. He is disappointed, true, but also hopeful that you mean what you say when you describe your overall interest in having a conjugal visit soon. Since you were so cool about making him feel desirable, the guy is still walking tall, loving life, and counting the minutes to your rendezvous!

Dish Panel

And now that you're well on your way to repossessing your warm, romantic, sensual persona, pay attention to my dishy dishers as they dish on about dish, er, *this*, topic.

Stacy: We make each other feel special on a daily basis.

We're not seen as being very romantic, but this is what we do to make each other feel special on a daily basis. Every time David calls, I answer the phone saying something like, "Hey, sweetheart" or some other pet name that comes to mind at the time. As for him to me, he'll stop and get me my "addiction" of Propel water. I am hopelessly addicted to that stuff! That's one of the biggest things that he does that makes me feel like I'm still very special to him.

Maggie: If nothing else we try to talk for a few minutes a day not about our child.

We have not mastered the art of keeping the romance alive (more like it sputters and spurts!). But if nothing else we try to make sure we talk for a few minutes each day about non-kid-related things! Actually, we were talking about how stay-at-home moms don't have job perks like "employed" workers, and my frugal husband actually said he thought getting a pedicure at the salon for the summer months would be a good perk for me. I have been going in for my pedicure each month and he has been so sweet about it!

Lisa: Dan and I seem to connect and click when we make each other laugh.

We are really not a baby-talk, sweetums kind of romantic couple. Long ago, we had friends who seemed to have forgotten one another's birth names, as they reverted to calling each other "Hon" all the time. (**"Hon**? Can you bring me the remote?" "Why sure, **Hon**!" "Gee . . . thanks, **Hon**!" *Ack!*) Dan and I seem to connect and click when we make each other laugh, especially by reminiscing about our college years, friends with funny quirks, and things no one else would find funny. Also, one of us will occasionally try to schedule a covert date night without the other knowing, and spring it on him/her at the last minute. Those are so much fun, especially the point when we're pulling out of the driveway, with the kids waving good-bye on the porch with

Grandma, and we realize we have a whole evening to hang out together! We did this one night during hockey playoffs several years ago, and just went up to a sports bar to hang out and watch the game. Woo hoo! *That's* romance!

Caroline: When we play this game we can engage in some really, umm, *intimate* activities.

With Jason (when we actually find the time) we do a variety of things:

1. Have a candlelit dinner after the kids are in bed. (We've done everything from nice juicy steaks to hefty bowls of mac n' cheese.)
2. Have nice long bubble baths together with the lights off and candles scattered around the bathroom.
3. My fave: play a board game called "Speak Love, Make Love." The game has many thought-provoking questions that help build up intimacy and trust (and possible lengthy conversations) and then, when you flip the board, you can engage in some really . . . ummm . . . intimate activities.

Brendalynn: A big favorite in my house is to not wear underwear while wearing a skirt.

To the average person all is well and normal, but he knows and yee-haw, he likes it!

Stephanie: What romance?

Funny you should ask, as this has been a serious problem for us in the past six months. Much of it is rooted in good old selfishness and how God wired men and women so differently. Sometimes we have a stay-at-home date. Mark brings home a yummy dessert, brews some tea, and we watch a grown-up movie (i.e., *not* animated or in a cover with primary colors). Sometimes the movies are real snoozers, but at least the dessert is good!

K: That always gets his engine running.

I will call and tell him I've been thinking about some of our past experiences and specifically which ones have been especially on my mind. *That* always gets his engine running!

GIGO

Be the Romantic One

We as women are always waiting for our men to make the first move, bring us flowers, chocolates, an incredibly sweet card. It's been awhile, hasn't it? And while we wait, we start to feel more and more discontent about whom we are married to. What happened to that thoughtful, sexy dude who seemed to overflow with little meaningful gestures? Well, you have a point there, but an equally valid argument is, what happened to you? When was the last time you bought him a fishing magazine, or picked up his favorite blueberry muffins from his favorite bakery, or gave him an incredibly sweet card?

I know, I know. You consider it a success these days when you buy essential groceries without your rambunctious toddler knocking over some sort of end cap display at the market. You don't have time to rummage through a magazine rack to pick out an outdoor periodical. And his favorite bakery is totally out of your way, and nowhere near Gymboree or preschool. Forget the card shop, because the last time you went in there your one-year-old broke three Christmas ornaments. You've let romance slide just like he has. Like sex therapist Valerie Davis Raskin suggests, you can become a romantic person again. It's good for you and him both, and possibly he may even pick up a few pointers and reciprocate. "The good news is that while you can't change other people, you can change yourself in ways that *invite* change in others."[1] Change it up, girl, and reintroduce romance into your life!

Ask yourself, "What did we used to have fun doing together?" Whether it's listening to live blues or playing putt-putt golf, try it again. A lot of times those activities have leftover magic in them. They serve as poignant reminders that yes, before you were scraping teething biscuit off your sweater and organizing his sock drawer, you were one-half of a romantic, swooning twosome who could hardly keep their hands off each other.

What Would Shulamith Do?

Shu who? Shulamith, Solomon's white-hot lover girl who burns up the pages of Song of Songs. Now she was one amorous chick. Consider her your role model when going about your daily routine. Would a romantic vixen such as Shulamith . . .

Floss her teeth in the presence of her lover?

Wear the sturdiest, biggest, most poly-blend granny panties known to womankind?

Garb herself in ripped, frayed sweat suits for night?

Okay, so Bible times predate polyester. My point is, quit being so comfortable around the man. "The comfortable ease of familiarity is a wonderful aspect of marriage," says Dr. Raskin, "but the intentionality of female mating rituals is a wonderful aspect of sexuality for both of you."[2] Shulamith loved Solomon and probably felt that sweet ease and relaxation that we feel when we are secure in a relationship. But I venture to guess she didn't get too comfy in matters of mating. She was quite intentional about putting the moves on King Sol. Take a page from Solomon and Shulamith's Song. Be purposefully romantic in the way you act and dress.

Turn Your Bedroom into the Chamber of Cha Cha Cha

Have kids taken over your space? It's time to repossess your bedroom as your own private love shack. To get rid of TV-watching kids in your bedroom, simply get rid of the TV. Ditch anything that reminds you of your obligations as a parent, say feng shui experts. Ban parenting books, school forms, and even pictures of your kids from your bedroom. This should be your space as a couple, not as parents, in order to spark some va va voom.

Leave your own intimate imprints on the room. Hang photos of the two of you, sans spawnlings, having a ball skiing or bowling or at a party. Honeymoon (first, second, or however many you've managed to sneak in) photos are good. Also, souvenirs from vacations or weekends or even day trips you've taken together underscore couplehood, not parenthood. We have an empty jar of fudge sauce from our twelfth anniversary at a chocolate themed B&B. The innkeeper, a graphic artist, custom made a label for the jar which reads, "Doyle and Lorilee, Chocolate 12th, Congratulations! November 9th, 2003." (And by the way, as of three days ago we have another, full jar of fudge sauce that says, "Doyle and Lorilee, Chocolate 15th, Congratulations! November 9th, 2006.")

Sweet little mementos like this are constant reminders that we have a love life, even though daily life sometimes begs to differ.

Also, stash some romantic items somewhere in the boudoir. Okay, so "boudoir" is currently a stretch. But once you toss out toys and add a few romantic goodies, it will start feeling less like Romper Room and more like the chamber of cha cha cha! Anyone, including your five-year-old, can see candles and silk pillows, but if you have anything racier, be sure and have an ironclad hiding place so your toddler doesn't find a thong and throw it in the toybox, only to be found by your mother-in-law next time she comes to babysit! (I can see the look on your face now, and it ain't pretty.)

Flirt

If you want to get in touch with your Inner Red-Hot Mama (IRHM), flirting is mandatory. Have winks, nudges, and double entendres flown out the (nursery) window? Guess what: the best moms in the world flirt in front of their kiddies. Why? Parental PDAs set an amazing example of how sweet and tender a marriage can be. So don't be shy about stealing a smooch or saying "I love you" when the kids are around. Bonus: those giggly grabs and suggestive looks will keep your mind and body constantly primed for the real fireworks to come. "The possible's slow fuse," said Emily Dickinson, "is lit by the imagination."

Just ask Ellie: "My husband and I will say little things in code to each other that are way over our four-year-old twins' heads," she dished. "Like, 'I received your *package* and I had to pay extra for shipping and *handling* because it was so big.' Of course we are busting a gut laughing and our kids think we are nuts. But they have no idea what's going on, and it totally gets us both in the mood."

Talk about "Tiramisu" a Lot

One way to flirt vigorously is to talk sexy every day. Tell him he's hot. Divulge the naughty idea you read about while standing in the checkout line. Reveal the fact that you can't wait to try it. Chatting up the possibility of a good time in bed will make both of you anticipate it more. All those little, cheeky utterances add up to the big setup. The more you talk it up, the more you want it to happen. In other words, sex is like dessert. After a whole week of eating heavy, rich dessert, it doesn't taste that great anymore. But when you think, talk, and dream of tiramisu for a few days, you can hardly wait to grab a dessert fork and satisfy your cravings!

Eight More Ways to Unleash Your IRHM

1. **Git 'er done.** Look at your lifestyle and think about what's getting in the way of you and the big man *knowing* each other in the biblical sense. Sexuality, the experts say, is a pattern, a mold, something that needs to happen on an ongoing basis or else other things will crowd it out. It's about behaving your way to success. Use it or lose it.

2. **Create warm welcomes.** You are totally warm and fuzzy wuzzy with your kids, and you slobber all over your dog—or cat ("Who's the cutest floppy-eared, fuzzy-wuzzy poochie poo?"). Intentionally greet your husband with the same enthusiasm. "Oh, but we're not a 'baby talk' kind of couple," you're protesting. Okay, fine, skip the cutesy nicknames. But do throw your arms around the man as if he's been fighting the Crimeans for years, not merely at Office Max picking up a printer cartridge. And then plant a big, warm, wet, sloppy one on the guy. He won't know what hit him, and those giggling kids will have a nice piece of evidence that Mommy and Daddy are *like this*. At the very least, try to kick up the zest in your voice when he walks through the door. It's an infinitely warmer hello than "Oh, it's you. Did you pick up a cartridge?" This kind of fuzzy wuzziness melts any lingering chill fast and also adds instant coziness to your marriage.

3. **Vroom! Start your date engines.** Tonight may not be date night, but try this quick trick, suggested by romance experts Leslie and Jimmy Caplan, to get excited about future weekend outings. First, each of you writes down two creative things to do; then the four ideas are sealed in separate envelopes. Now one of you chooses an envelope—and your destiny for the weekend to come.

4. **Behind locked doors.** Find an excuse to go behind a locked door in the middle of the day. Tell the kids Mom and Dad have to discuss something privately. *In the shower.* Make sure the pint-sized interlopers are well occupied with a movie and snacks. And then for heaven's sake, lock the

door! Nothin' says lovin' like a good quickie, so sneak it in whenever you can.

5. **Pop a quiz.** Interview your sweetie via email once a week. Why? "Most couples, even those who are already very close, are more likely to express a deeper side of themselves in a written note rather than orally," says Michael Webb, founder of a romance-building website. Webb recommends shooting off one of these getting-to-know-you-even-better cues: "What first attracted you to me?" "Do you ever crave a quickie? When?" or "What are the three most sensitive places on your body?"

6. **Touch.** Running your fingers through his hair (or rubbing his bald spot), hugging, kissing, holding hands, cuddling—any kind of touching will make you feel good. In fact, touching increases a feel-fab hormone called oxytocin, which truly brings about a feeling of well-being. Scared he might take your touchy-feely ways as a come-on? Be straight with your guy and tell him touching is good for your sex drive—in the long run.

7. **Help him succeed.** Don't sabotage the whole plan by acting like your husband is your female friend. What I mean is, how well will he do if all you say is, "I need you to be more romantic if you want more sex." Be specific whenever you can. Help him out by asking for what you want in terms of relationship, romance, and of course between the sheets.

I have found success in presenting my dear one with a page ripped out of a catalog or flyer featuring one or more things that might interest me as gifts. "I would be thrilled if you got me anything on this page for Valentine's Day," I might say. This conveys a few key facts, such as that a present would be sweet and romantic (and expected) for Valentine's Day (insert your gift-giving occasion), that I am hoping for such a thing, and that he will be absolutely successful in his endeavor to please me should he pluck some trinket off that page!

"Ask him to stop and pick up fresh flowers and then tell him how charming it is to see him walk through the door with a bouquet, even though it was your idea in the first place," says Dr. Raskin in her book *Great Sex for Moms*. "Request that he make reservations at a romantic restaurant and couple the request with the local newspaper's Valentine's Day restaurant guide."[3]

8. **Ask him to seduce you and chances are he'll say yes.** Give your man this mission and he'll choose to accept it: "Do whatever you can in your own power to make me want to have sex with you by Friday night." This puts him in the role of seducer, and he'll probably be doing cartwheels to woo you. It's playful, flirty, and win-win. "He gets out of the supplicant role; you get the attention you appreciate and a glimpse of your old boyfriend," says Raskin.[4]

The Eight Best Things You Can Do to Rev Up Your Relationship

1. Put your relationship with your husband first, and your kids second.

Now, now . . . before you throw tomatoes at me, try to keep an open mind. I know it sounds odd to suggest that your husband—a grown-up, able-to-cut-his-own-meat, doesn't-need-a-car-seat man—should take precedence over a 48-pound, needs-his-crusts-cut-off, drinks-from-a-sippy-cup child.

It seems like the most natural thing in the world to make our precious little ones our first priority. Our emotional alliances shift almost the minute we become mothers, fundamentally changing who we feel we are. We love our babies with a consuming intensity that can shut out everyone and everything else—girlfriends, career interests, and yes, the love of our lives. He gets relegated to the back of the bus, so to speak, in terms of our attentions and energies.

Lisa: I think the reason I do focus on the kids more is that I look at raising them as primarily my job—my self-worth is tied up in what type of human beings they turn out to be.

Tenny: I know that after being with the kids all day, and putting their needs in front of my own, it's just natural to put their needs in front of my husband's. I know this is not a good choice, but usually logical and in sync with what's happened during the day.

Julie: I didn't realize I was putting the kids ahead of my husband, but he had said I was. Both times he complained about this, we had a newborn (it's an obvious given to me that a newborn is going to be a time zapper).

Maggie: When I am done being Mommy, I want to go curl up and read, go to the bookstore, take a bubble bath, knit . . . Sometimes I want time alone more than time with my husband, and it is not because I don't love him. Relationships take energy, and so much energy goes into parenting.

Evidently, it's common for moms to give dads a far littler slice of the time and energy pie than they give the little pie gobblers. Lisa said her self-worth was tied up in how the kids turned out. Tenny remarked that it was all too natural to fall into the kids-first pattern after being RoboMommy all day. Julie cited the time crunch, while

Meg confessed that she was out of verve by the time her toddler-chasing day was done. Their true confessions are typical: Two-thirds of new moms say that the person they feel most emotionally connected to right now is their baby. Oddly, the majority of dads say the person they feel connected to is their wife!

Something is off-kilter there. As natural and easy as it is to slip into the kid-ruled life, we have to consciously and intentionally make our husbands a priority, even the main concern, in our relationship pizza. This doesn't mean letting your baby's diaper drag on the floor because it hasn't been changed, or allowing your children to play with knives in the backyard so you can have a romantic candlelit dinner with your husband. But start giving your marriage the credence it deserves.

Quit overfeeding the kids and throwing your husband the sliver of you left at the end. The strongest couples do little things to convey to each other—and the kids—how much they value each other. They shift their attention to each other sometimes, like Gail and Jason: "We let our kids know we aren't going to drop everything when they want our attention—which is always," she said. "We don't let them interrupt our chats if they are not really in urgent need of something. They are learning that, with a few exceptions, they have to wait their turn to talk."

Balanced couples set early bedtimes and firm policies about the kids not jumping out of bed every five minutes after they've been tucked in. Once the kids are in their rooms and out of your hair, you can breathe, finish your sentences, and maybe even canoodle a little!

On the same wavelength, encourage your kids' independence by teaching them how to do for themselves. This means Junior can pour his own drink the next time your husband is telling you about his day, and even smear and smush his own PB&J together. Yes, he'll make a mess, but in the long run you'll have carved out another five minutes together.

Remember how Julie said her man called her on her kid-centeredness? She found a way to reverse that and focus on him more: "Now I make sure that I make a big deal of him coming home, have dinner ready (even if it's grilled cheese), listen to his work woes," she said. "I never realized that this mattered so much to men. I didn't think they even noticed if we were preoccupied. I guess I was wrong."

Finally, listen to two moms who get a gold star from me for their deliberate attempts to make the hubster number one:

Stacy: David works anywhere from sixty-five to eighty hours a week. When he comes home, I tend to focus all my attention on him. Don't get me wrong, my kids still get attention, but I don't feel like I put them before David. I feel that if it weren't for him, and our love, I wouldn't have the pleasure of being their mother to begin with.

K: I am one of those odd women who actually puts Dad ahead of the kids, at least when he is home! I stay at home, so I guess I feel since they get my undivided attention all day, when Dad gets home he deserves some special attention.

2. Do little things.

Duos who still have the hots for each other spark up those heated feelings in tiny, seemingly mundane ways, like Catharine: "We don't really do anything romantic for each other," she said. "We do more of the practical little things—like emptying the dishwasher before the other person knows or can get to it or getting a late-night snack for one another after our little one is in bed." Keep your eyes peeled and your ears open for ways to make him feel valued and cared for. Hand him a hot towel when he steps out of the shower. Pour him more coffee before his mug is empty. Play his favorite game—even if it's pool and you're a Monopoly kind of gal. Fix him the meal he loves that you can't stand. Wear the sweater he bought you to a family function; show it off and tell everyone he bought it. (Okay, it has chickens on it. You only really have to wear it once.)

Surprise him in the shower one morning, not by gracing him with your in-the-buff presence, although hopefully you are doing that anyway. This time, shock him by thinning out the seventeen hair and body products that clutter the shower ledge and stock it instead with a manly shampoo with no frou frou fragrance.

"What? And give up my bodifying/renewing/clarifying/shine-enhancing shampoo, conditioner, color booster, and glaze?"

You are sputtering, I know. What, do you think I'm crazy? Just put all that girlie stuff in a basket by the tub. Don't ditch it, for heaven's sake—move it and make room for his lonely only hair product. He'll be thrilled, and he won't waft with a miasma of raspberries, mangoes, and peaches next time he's in a meeting with his boss.

You get my point. Small kindnesses, doled out regularly, will make your guy feel prized. Bonus: He may very well catch on to your wily ways and pay it forward with his own love-boosting moves.

3. Fuel your own interests.

Do your own thing on a regular basis, and let him do his. You might be thinking, *Well, yeah. Chapter 2 was totally about that. Why are you whacking us over the head with it one more time?*

Because carving out time spent apart (i.e., individual time off), invigorates a pair like crazy. Absence makes the heart grow fonder, or in other words, more affectionate, doting, and tender.

You know that old saying, "How can I miss you if you don't go away?" Doing things independently gives you a chance to connect the dots your guy can't connect for you. Say one of you is energized by basketball, the other one feels soothed and charmed at the ballet. I'm not saying which one, but perhaps you can take a stab at guessing, not to be too old school here. Maybe you love the Bulls, and he has a yen for Swan Lake.

I'm just saying, for Pete's sake, do something that brings you to your happy place, and then go home rejuvenated, brimming with reports of foul shots or pirouettes gone amok ("And then the swan squashed the tuba player in the orchestra pit . . .").

Separate outings give you more to talk about and naturally bring fresh energy to your home and relationship. Make space for each other to pursue your own hobbies and interests. You'll fill in the oh-so-personal blanks you need filled, and he'll do the same. When you both get your "me" time, you'll feel good and that positive vigor will overflow into your union.

4. Compliment your man.

Everywhere in your relationship, that is! When you tell your man he looks good in that shirt, or he makes the fluffiest pancakes on the planet, it charges the atmosphere around you with good stuff. You may be in the kitchen when you tell him he's a great dad, or he's sweet or funny or smart, but whatever humdrum place you're standing in is transformed. The air clears and the vibe changes. Make sure your accolades are sincere, but do make it a point of training your brain to pick up on his pros whenever you can. Why? Focusing on and noticing the good qualities in the world around you give your mood a boost all by itself. Also, couples who talked about positive aspects of their relationships reduced stress by 15 percent, while those who talked about the negatives increased their stress by 48 percent, in a study conducted by the *Journal of Family Psychology*.

Do the math. Experts also say that paying little tributes to your mate pays off for you too. "People benefit from being the objects of compliments, but you also benefit being givers of them. Recipients benefit from knowing that you notice and learn that you value them.

So compliments are powerful in motivating continued efforts. People strive to do more of what brings praise from others."[1]

5. Get away *a deux* for a day, a weekend, or more.

The tightest twosomes find creative ways to leave the building as a couple, not parents, on a regular basis. This means taking charge of your schedule and not letting your schedule take charge of you. It means chiseling out chunks of time to be the goin'-on team you always knew you could be.

If you both work, schedule a vacation or personal day together and then spend it together, relaxing together at home with the kids in their usual places. Have breakfast and lunch out, or simply enjoy the peace and quiet a kid-free house gives you. If your work gives you sick time for doctor's appointments, schedule your annual check-ups on the same afternoon and rendezvous later for a latte. It'll still feel like a little bit of hooky!

Once every couple of weeks, jot date night on your calendar. You don't have to go hot air ballooning and picnic with champagne and brie. Even hot dogs at a baseball game will taste like heaven when it's just you and him.

Doyle and I have had some wonderful evenings spent at Schuler's, our local bookstore/café. We have a salad or sandwich for dinner and then he roams the music and I stroll amongst the books. Every so often we hook up and compare notes, or show each other some treasure we've found. Sometimes we just have a cuppa java and sit across from each other, flipping through magazines. So we're not having profound, life-altering conversations every single time. Who cares? We're together, and somehow it's bonding. It's a cheap date, especially if we don't buy new books and CDs!

Brainstorm what a great date would look like to you. Scribble three ideas for outings that you would love, and then have your guy do the same. Shuffle and stick them in an envelope, then take turns picking notions for a nifty night out.

Call up Grandma and Grandpa if they live nearby, or swap portions of time with another young family. Get a membership at a gym with tyke-care, and then get sweaty together as the youngsters make new pals and play.

And every so often, plan a trip away together, even for a weekend. Often it's the planning and dreaming that truly fuses two people. We are still reaping the benefits of our time together in Costa Rica when Jonah was two, and I recall with fondness all the evenings at Schuler's, poring over travel guides to that lush, beautiful little country.

You may not have dough right this instant to go gallivanting off to Tahiti or someplace, but imagining where you might like to go if you could is worthwhile. Browse in your local bookstore's travel aisle, and each of you choose the top five places you'd like to visit. Later, sit down and go over your fantasy destinations together. Discover you've got one in common? You just took the first step toward making a shared dream come true.

6. Give each other gifts.

Don't wait for his birthday or Christmas to gift him with a little *somethin', somethin'*. Launch a new tradition in your household in which you two exchange gifts every other Wednesday or some such deal. Or maybe monthly on, perhaps, the month-i-versary of your wedding. That would make it quite easy to remember, plus ensure you do it once a month. My dad got my mom a card or flowers or some little trinket on the twelfth of each month, to commemorate in a small yet meaningful way the vows they spoke on September 12, 1964. When my dad died, the florist whose shop was right beside his bookstore said she and her employees all referred to my dad as "Orchid Abe" because he so faithfully ordered simple, inexpensive bouquets of white orchids for my mom. At his funeral, the florist sent a vase of white orchids, and the card read, "We'll miss you, Orchid Abe." Sweet, eh? My parents' marriage was close-knit, loving, and durable. Those little month-i-versaries, countless cards, and innumerable white orchids were among the reasons why.

Why gifts? When you give a token of love to someone, it conveys a sense of caring and thoughtfulness, even if the present itself is pretty standard. But the more time passes, the more imaginative you will probably be in your gift giving. You might give him a bag of his favorite candies one month, nestled in a gift basket with coupons good for a back rub or maybe something a little hotter. And then one month, a bright idea will pop into your head that will blow his mind, something so personal, so no-one-gets-you-like-I-do, that he'll fall in love all over again. Gifts are like little windows into someone's inmost self. They show the recipient that you care, that you are deeply invested in them, and that you know them incredibly well.

Too much pressure to come up with the perfect, unforgettable gift? Don't sweat it. Just start small, with a six-dollar guitar magazine that he doesn't subscribe to but would if it were cheaper, or a fun yet impractical fishing lure. And don't get discouraged if he comes up with something sort of lame the first few times. The point is, you want to get to know him more deeply, to laugh at inside jokes, to make inroads into each other's sometimes secret selves.

Shhh, don't tell Doyle, but I am planning a little surprise for him: a Doyle bobblehead venerating his days as the center for the Reeths Puffer Rockets football squad, circa 1986. I saw the custom bobblehead idea in *Family Fun* magazine, so it's actually designed as a project for children. (Hopefully I can do it, in that case. I'm not just craft "challenged," my **MOPS** group makes me sit at the "special needs" craft table!) Anyway, it will feature his photo, his number, and his school colors. It's a gift that will say, "I know you loved your football days, and you miss them all the time. Here's a little reminder of those glory days and a way to say 'Go Rockets!' forever!"

Julie talks about her husband's best gift: "How many ways would you melt if your husband went to the local antique shop, purchased a three-dollar skeleton key, and presented it as 'the key to his heart'? Just ask Nick how many ways he heard thank you from me for that one."

7. Do something you love together.

If Doyle and I could find an activity we love to share, then anyone can. I used to tell people, mostly serious, that the only thing my husband and I had in common was a mortgage, a dog, and oh yes, three children. He's a burly outdoorsman who lives to snag fish and hunt deer, and I'm a city girl, born and bred, who gets chills (the good kind) whenever I get to walk Chicago's Magnificent Mile, stopping here and there for foufy coffee at an outdoor café. I adore hockey, he's stuck on football. I'm newfangled, he's old school. Canadian/American. Lefty/righty. Musicals/plays. Romance/action. And the list goes on . . . forever!

How'd we ever hook up? Good question, although I do know he had really blue eyes and brilliant white teeth in college. Still does, actually, though cerulean peepers and lustrous bicuspids only serve to advance a relationship so far.

But somehow we have found a communal passion, a shared interest that we love to pursue—together! It's rock 'n' roll, baby. That's right. Music is our common ground. This doesn't mean we like the same bands or artists—no ho. On our tenth anniversary we took in the Rock and Roll Hall of Fame together and argued over where we would spend more time, in the John Lennon exhibit or the Jimi Hendrix shrine. I poked fun of Jimi's pointy pink shoes (How could Doyle, who doesn't even wear *faded red* clothing, condone such flaky footwear?), and he rolled his eyes at John and Yoko's "bed-in" peace protest. But we had a ball anyway, checking out all the sequined jumpsuits and Fender guitars.

We both gravitate to behind-the-scenes rock documentaries on cable, and we'll buy each other CDs we think the other will like. Because of my moonlighting gig as an entertainment reporter, Doyle gets to tag along with me to all sorts of blues, rock, pop, folk, and country concerts too. Some of our closest times have been driving home from a show, discussing this band's cheesy lead singer or that bass player's astonishing solo.

Against all odds, two firm opposites like me and the big guy found a parallel passion.

Against all odds, two firm opposites like me and the big guy found a parallel passion. You can too. Food, books, music, gardening, kayaking—there's a world of pursuits to choose from, and chances are you'll share one of them. There's nothing like it for unifying your little club of two.

Listen to the things that make other couples thrive:

Kerith and Amani—Gardening: There's something about working in the dirt and digging things up that grounds us. When we're outside, we don't hear the phone, we're not on the computer—it's just us.

Kristen and Kristofer—Scrabble: Last year we realized we were spending a lot of our time together watching TV . . . Now Sunday-night Scrabble is an almost weekly ritual. We're both competitive, which is fun, and we play for bragging rights. I can see us when we're old, sitting around playing together.

John and Kim—the dogs: Most nights after work we take them for a walk, which is a great way to reconnect. And we have a blast doing little things like bathing them or playing fetch. They definitely inject fun in our relationship.[2]

8. Realize it won't be this hard forever.

One of the great paradoxes of our lives as moms is that one day all the diapers, tantrums, and sleep deprivation will be gone, and then—perverse creatures!—we'll miss them. Okay, so we won't actually miss poop or screaming fits or walking around like something out of *Night of the Living Dead*, but in the haze of time passing we'll feel pangs for footie pjs, sleeping angels, and cozy bedtime stories. And then we'll wonder why we thought it was so hard back then.

But listen to me here, girls (I'm mentally grabbing you by your lapels): *It is hard, here and now.* The demands of parenthood are bottomless. But someday it will get easier, quieter, and more peaceful around the family casa. The most robust and resilient partners are the ones that grasp the fleetingness of this epoch with little ones running around. If you can appreciate that the taxing, testing days of your marriage, under siege some days, it seems, are short term, you'll cope that much better.

Feeling out of sync with your man in this kiddie-intense daze is going to happen—every day. But it doesn't mean you're headed for splitsville. If you're irritated or frustrated or feeling trapped, it's time to hang back a little, assess the most vital relationship of your life, and make a greater effort to link up with your guy.

Make your mindset this: Yes, parenting is hard, and marriage even harder, but it's also worth it. This grand adventure called raising kids is a huge and incredibly meaningful endeavor, one you're undertaking with the love of your life.

The kid drama will die down, and then it's just you and him. What will your relationship look like then? The answer lies in what you give, starting now. There is something to be prized about this era of marriage in the midst of being Mom and Dad, a precious quality of protecting that spark while you're hosing down a toddler covered in spaghetti sauce.

It's right there in the mundane, the chaotic, the routine, and the crazy. You'll see what I mean the next time you catch his eye over the tousled head of your child, and smile because the kid just said something unbearably cute or outrageous. Or when you gingerly hand off your drowsy baby for your husband to tuck in. You'll understand when, some night soon, you are both lazing around on the couch after the kids have been tucked in, and you notice his lopsided grin can still make your heart flutter just a little. In a moment like that, you'll know that what you have together is unspeakably precious. And you'll be right.

Conclusion

So, dear reader, we have come to the end of our little minivan whirl together, exploring those bumpy pathways of marriage plus kids. Throughout writing this book I have been struck again and again with how much I am in the trenches with y'all. Every day I face one of the hot-button issues described here, whether it be differences in the way Doyle and I discipline our kids (and with a wild and crazy now-two-year-old, there are heaps of opportunities), tension over who gets a night off, or friction regarding a money matter. It's important for me to always keep it real, and I want you to know I don't have it all together (at least that was true as of five minutes ago). Maybe someday soon I will have achieved the perfectly balanced marriage and family life, but I doubt it. Even the Red-Hot Mama thing, which is my specialty since I write and speak about it so often, can get a big wet blanket thrown on it in the form of inconvenient kid drama, hormones, sleep deprivation, you name it. But I do think that gathering other moms' stories and collecting all of this research and advice has helped me in my marriage. I hope it has helped you too.

Sometimes, when I am really at a low ebb in my relationship with Doyle, when I think that parenting will eventually rob us of every romantic thought we ever had about each other, I remember my parents' marriage, and I hang on tighter. I wrote about half of this book after my dad died in July 2006, and at the time I wondered how I could write an intermittently funny book on marriage when I was in so much pain. What fueled my writing then was my parents' relationship. I wanted to honor it in this book through a few memories, but mostly through honoring marriage itself. At the end of my dad's life, what left a great impression on me was his love for my mom and her love for him. When my mom asked him if he was ready to go to heaven, he said something that may sound shocking or even slightly un-churchy. "No," my dad said, holding my mom's hand and crying. "I want to stay here with you."

At the end of the day, when the dust of kid drama and the challenges of raising little ones settles, I want that kind of love, that type of endurance. So I will wake up tomorrow, and the mom-and-dad marriage negotiations will start all over again. We'll try to work it out, and sometimes we'll fail. We'll laugh at stupid stuff no one else thinks is funny, and through it all we'll try to keep the kids fed, bathed, and off the highway. And we will keep trying to rev up that metaphorical minivan, the symbol of love in the midst of family craziness. Hopefully, we'll see you on the same road someday.

Notes

Chapter 1: Mom's the Bad Guy and Dad's the Softie, or Vice Versa

1. Fred Rogers, "Different Parenting Styles," http://pbskids.org/rogers/parentsteachers/theme/1621_p_art.html.

2. Ibid.

Chapter 2: The Time-Off Tug-o-War

1. "Conquering . . . Differing Attitudes about Discipline," *Ladies Home Journal*, www.lhj.com/lhj/story.jhtml?storyid=/templatedata/lhj/story/data/16534.xml.

Chapter 3: I Am Mama, Hear Me Roar

1. Read more about this in Cathy Young, "The Mama Lion at the Gate: Maternal Chauvinism Is a Dad's Greatest Obstacle to Parental Parity," Salon.com, June 12, 2000, http://archive.salon.com/mwt/feature/2000/06/12/gatekeeping/.

2. "Does This Sound like You? Here's What You Said: Does Hubby Do a Good Job of Filling In for You?" http://mommasaid.net/kitchentable.aspx.

3. Sheri and Bob Stritof, "Maternal Gatekeeping" Press Release, http://marriage.about.com/cs/roles/a/maternalgate_5.htm.

4. Ibid.

5. Armin Brott, "Eight Things Women Can Do to Get Fathers More Involved," http://mrdad.com/qa/justformom/8-things.htm.

6. Ibid.

Chapter 4: I'll Do the Dishes and You Wash the Cat

1. Armin Brott, "Eight Things Women Can Do."
2. Ibid.

Chapter 5: Homicide Is Not the Answer

1. Lambeth Hochwald, "Marriage Makeover: We Have In-Law Issues," http://www.redbookmag.com/print-this/love/marriage-makeover-inlaws-ll.
2. Geoff Williams, "Dad's Side: When Grandma Knows It All," *BabyTalk*, http://www.parenting.com/parenting/article/0,19840,1175606,00.html.

Chapter 7: Money, Money, Money

1. Martha Baer, "It's Not About the Benjamins," *Tango*, September/ October 2006, 48.

Chapter 8: When Your Ovaries Twitch at the Sight of Footie PJs

1. Clare Lissaman and Stephen Israel, "The Story of Lily," *Parents*, October 2006, 96.
2. Gary and Carrie Oliver, "What About Me-Time?" *Marriage Partnership*, Summer 2006, http://www.christianitytoday.com/mp/2006/002/17.18.html.

Chapter 9: Get It Goin' On Again, Sister Friend

1. Valerie Davis Raskin, *Great Sex for Moms: Ten Steps to Nurturing Passion While Raising Kids* (New York: Fireside, 2002), 127.
2. Ibid.
3. Ibid., 129.
4. Ibid.

Chapter 10: The Eight Best Things You Can Do to Rev Up Your Relationship

1. Hara Estroff Marano, "The Art of Flattery: Free gifts of love: How to give and receive compliments with grace," *True U Magazine*, http://www.true.com/magazine/dating_compliments.htm.
2. Julia Dahl, "The Thing That Makes Our Relationship Thrive," *Redbook*, July 2006, 132.

About MOPS

You take care of your children, mom. Who takes care of you? MOPS International (Mothers of Preschoolers) encourages, equips, and develops mothers of preschoolers to be the best moms they can be.

MOPS is dedicated to the message that "better moms make a better world" and understands that moms of young children need encouragement during these critical and formative years. Chartered MOPS groups meet in approximately 4,000 churches and Christian ministries throughout the United States and 24 other countries. Each MOPS group helps mothers find friendship and acceptance, provides opportunities for women to develop and practice leadership skills in a group, and promotes spiritual growth. MOPS groups are chartered ministries of local churches and meet at a variety of times and locations: daytime, evenings, and on weekends; in churches, homes, and workplaces.

The MOPPETS program offers a loving, learning experience for children while their moms attend MOPS.

Other quality **MOPS** resources include *MomSense* magazine, **MOPS** books available at the www.MOPShop.org, website forums, and events.

With 14.3 million mothers of preschoolers in the United States alone, many moms can't attend a **MOPS** group. However, these moms still need the mothering support that **MOPS** International can offer! For a small registration fee, any mother of a preschooler can join the **MOPS** International Membership and receive *MomSense* magazine (6 times a year), a weekly MOM-E-Mail of encouragement, and other valuable benefits.

Get Connected!
www.MOPS.org

Lorilee Craker is the author of nine books, including *When the Belly Button Pops, the Baby's Done,* and *A Is for Atticus: Baby Names from the Great Books.* She is also a frequent speaker at MOPS groups and other mom events, and she moonlights as an entertainment reporter for the *Grand Rapids Press.* Mostly she is the proud wife and mother of a family that includes husband Doyle, three children, a dog, and two unruly kittens.

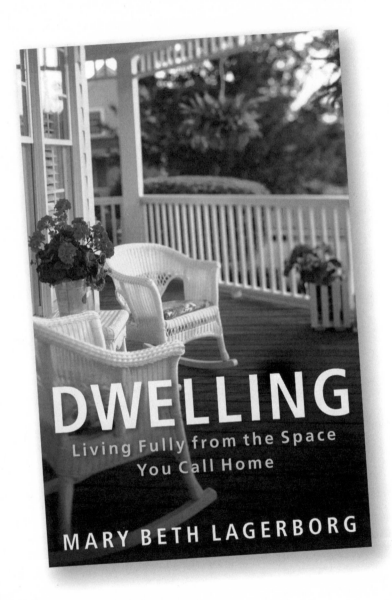

R Revell
a division of Baker Publishing Group
www.revellbooks.com

ONE TOUGH Mother

It's Time to Step Up and Be the Mom

Julie Barnhill

Mothers of Preschoolers
www.MOPS.org